HEROES OF HISTORY

MERIWETHER LEWIS

Off the Edge of the Map

HEROES OF HISTORY

MERIWETHER LEWIS

Off the Edge of the Map

JANET & GEOFF BENGE

Emerald Books

P.O. BOX 635, LYNNWOOD, WA 98046

Emerald Books are distributed through YWAM Publishing. For a full list of titles, including other great biographies, visit our website at www.ywampublishing.com or call 1-800-922-2143.

Library of Congress Cataloging-in-Publication Data

Benge, Janet, 1958-
    Meriwether Lewis : off the edge of the map / Janet and Geoff Benge.
        p. cm. -- (Heroes of history)
Includes bibliographical references.
Summary: A biography of the co-leader of the 1804-1806 Lewis and Clark expedition into the unmapped American West, including his early life and the formation of the Corps of Discovery.
    ISBN 1-883002-80-X (alk. paper)
    1. Lewis, Meriwether, 1774-1809--Juvenile literature.
2. Explorers--West (U.S.)--Biography--Juvenile literature. 3. Lewis and Clark Expedition (1804-1806)--Juvenile literature. 4. West (U.S.)--Discovery and exploration--Juvenile literature. 5. West (U.S.)--Description and travel--Juvenile literature. [1. Lewis, Meriwether, 1774-1809. 2. Explorers. 3. Lewis and Clark Expedition (1804-1806) 4. West (U.S.)--Discovery and exploration.] I. Benge, Geoff, 1954- II. Title.
        F592.7.L42 B46 2001
        917.804'2'092--dc21

                                                2001005054

Meriwether Lewis: Off the Edge of the Map
Copyright © 2001 by Janet and Geoff Benge

10 09 08 07 06 05 04 03 02 01   10 9 8 7 6 5 4 3 2 1

Published by Emerald Books
P.O. Box 635
Lynnwood, Washington 98046

ISBN 1-883002-80-X

Printed in the United States of America.

HEROES OF HISTORY
Biographies

George Washington Carver
Meriwether Lewis
Abraham Lincoln
William Penn
George Washington

More Heroes of History coming soon!
Unit study curriculum guides are available
for these biographies.

Available at your local bookstore or
through Emerald Books
1 (800) 922-2143

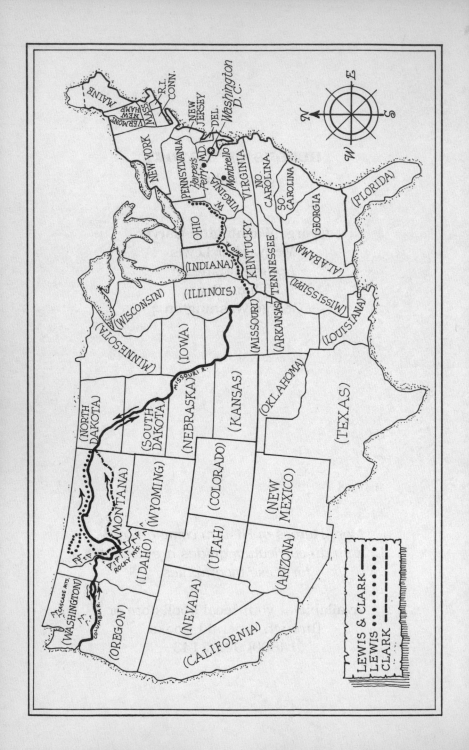

Contents

Chapter 1

Off the Edge
of the Map

Here boy," Meriwether Lewis called as he stood on the edge of the bluff. Scannon, his faithful Newfoundland dog, raced toward him with a squirrel firmly locked in his teeth and his tail wagging eagerly.

"Good boy!" Meriwether said, patting the dog's enormous head.

After petting the dog for a few moments, Meriwether turned his attention to the sparkling ribbon of water below—the Missouri River, which meandered its way across the Great Plains of North America. On either side of the river the land stretched unbroken to the horizon. Despite the vast vista before him, Meriwether was focused on the nine boats on the river. Three, a keelboat and two canoes, were headed downstream to St. Louis carrying precious cargo—all the plant and animal specimens collected, maps drawn, and notes written during the yearlong expedition up the Missouri River to this point. The items were eventually bound for President Jefferson himself. But although this important cargo was on its way downriver, Meriwether's attention focused specifically on the six dugout canoes and two pirogues making their way in the opposite direction. This was the next stage of the expedition, which was headed farther on up the Missouri River. If all went well, it would cross the Rocky Mountains and make it all the way to the Pacific Ocean.

As Meriwether watched the expedition—which he had helped plan and was co-leader of—move upstream, he wondered if Christopher Columbus or Captain Cook felt as he did as their ships left port and set course for unexplored waters. Certainly the canoes and pirogues were no substitute for the breathtaking sight of a vessel under full sail, but Meriwether felt a surge of pride and exhilaration at the sight of them on their way upriver into unimaginable adventures. The thirty-two-member Corps of Discovery that made up the expedition was not casting itself out into unmapped oceans as had Cook's and Columbus's men. It was headed into a two-thousand-mile-wide swath of land no white person had set foot on. Everything the explorers depended on for life either was aboard their boats or would have to be found along the way.

Mixed in with the exhilaration of adventure were some doubts and fears. What would happen to them all in the year ahead? Would they survive? Would they make it to their destination? Would Indian attacks or encounters with grizzly bears or other animals turn them back? Would the Missouri River itself prove to be a friend or foe? These nagging questions had no answers. Only time would tell. The Corps of Discovery was about to travel off the edge of the map into Terra Incognita, the unknown lands.

As Meriwether walked along the top of the bluff on his way to catch up to the expedition, he thought about growing up in Virginia and on the frontier of Georgia. All his life he had craved adventure. Even as a small child he had been more daring, more foolhardy, and more courageous than his brothers or cousins. And now here he was, leading the ultimate American adventure—to cross the North American continent overland. He was headed for an adventure far removed from the genteel life of a plantation owner for which as a young man he had been groomed.

Chapter 2

A Fearless Young Man

Five year old Meriwether Lewis had been saying good-bye to his father as far back as he could remember. Today, a cold, wet day in November 1779, Meriwether once again stood at the window waving proudly as his father, William, rode off to fight against the British for American independence.

Meriwether was born on August 18, 1774, nine months after the Boston Tea Party. The Declaration of Independence was signed when he was two years old, and so it seemed normal to him that his father should be away fighting. Whenever William Lewis came home on leave, he always had fascinating tales to tell his son. This time he told Meriwether about how General John Sullivan had invaded Iroquois territory with 3,700 Continental soldiers and driven the Iroquois all the way into Canada.

During this visit Meriwether overheard his father telling his mother that he thought the Continental forces were gaining ground in the struggle for independence, though the British were not yet ready to surrender.

"Mama says it's time for lunch," said Jane, Meriwether's nine-year-old sister.

Meriwether took one last look at the distant figure of his father and followed Jane to the dining room. Two-year-old Reuben toddled along behind him.

"I wish he'd waited. It's raining hard out there," said Meriwether's mother, Lucy.

"Go ahead and eat something. You'll fret away to nothing if you don't eat. William has survived a lot worse than a rainstorm," Meriwether's grandmother told Lucy.

Lucy Lewis picked up a biscuit and slowly spread butter on it. "As soon as the weather improves, I have to tend to old Widow Durham. I hear she ripped her leg open bringing in firewood. It's badly swollen. A warm poultice should help her," she said.

"What would you put in the poultice?" Meriwether asked. Even at five years of age he was fascinated by the way his mother used herbs, bark, and leaves to cure people.

His mother smiled and ruffled his light brown hair. "Oh, Meriwether, I think you'll do doctoring one day just like me. Let me see. For an infection I'd use crushed marigolds, garlic, and honey.

"Just like you used on Mr. Taylor's arm," Meriwether said.

His mother nodded.

After lunch Meriwether played house with Jane while Reuben did his best to disrupt them, just as he always did. The rain continued to beat down steadily on the shingle roof.

It was just getting dark when there was a loud thump at the front door. It was unusual for someone to visit so late, and Meriwether watched keenly as a servant went to investigate.

"Oh, my gracious, it's the master," the servant wailed.

Meriwether gasped as the door swung wide open and his father collapsed on the Persian rug. William Lewis was covered in mud, and one of his boots was missing.

Meriwether heard a swish of skirts on the wooden floor as his mother and grandmother came running.

"What happened?" Lucy asked as she helped her husband onto one of the wooden chairs.

"I lost my horse," Mr. Lewis whispered. "I got to Secretary's Ford on the Rivanna River. The water was high, but I thought I could make it across. I was near the middle when a log hit the horse. I managed to get back to shore, but the horse was swept downstream. I walked back here."

William Lewis slumped in the chair, exhausted from the effort of talking. He was carried upstairs, where he was washed and put to bed. By the morning, ominous coughing was coming from the room, and Lucy was preparing a special herb vapor. The word *pneumonia* was being whispered among the servants.

The following morning the house was silent. William Lewis had died. Meriwether could scarcely take in what had happened. He wondered why a strong man like his father had died from getting wet crossing a river. His mind whirred, searching for an answer as he watched the funeral procession wind its way to the small family cemetery at Cloverfields. Cloverfields was his grandparents' plantation where they had been staying. The Lewises owned a neighboring plantation ten miles away, but it was impossible to return his father's body there because of the bad weather.

Though he was unaware of it at that moment, on his father's death Meriwether inherited the family plantation, named Locust Hill. In America at the time primogeniture was practiced. This meant that when a man died, everything he owned—land, slaves, livestock, and money—became the sole property of the oldest son instead of being divided equally among the surviving wife and children. At five years of age, Meriwether Lewis, as the oldest son, became the owner of the 2,000-acre Locust Hill plantation, 520 pounds in cash, 24 slaves, and 147 gallons of whiskey.

Nicholas Lewis, William Lewis's older brother, was put in charge of the Locust Hill estate until Meriwether was old enough to run it himself. Meriwether liked his Uncle Nick, as did just about everyone else in Albemarle County, Virginia. After the death of his father, Meriwether began to spend a lot of time with his uncle.

Soon after William Lewis's death, another man became an important part of Meriwether's life. His name was Captain John Marks, and he came to call on Mrs. Lewis. No one was surprised when six months later, in May 1780, Lucy Lewis announced she was going to marry Captain Marks. The two were a good match. Captain Marks had a medical discharge from the Continental army and wanted to settle down with a wife, while Lucy needed a man like him around to support her and help her raise the children, especially since she had no money or belongings of her own.

After the wedding on May 13, 1780, John Marks moved into Locust Hill. Meriwether liked his new stepfather. It was especially comforting to have him around when the Revolutionary War struck close to home. The British commander, General Charles Cornwallis, sent Colonel Tarleton to destroy as much property in Albemarle County as possible. Meriwether was spared most of the details of these cruel raids, though he could see the tall plumes of black smoke rising on the horizon as plantations were torched. He often overheard the slaves whispering about the "evil goings on" of the Red Coats (British soldiers).

Under orders from Colonel Tarleton, British troops were to gather up what crops they could and destroy the rest. Hundreds of thousands of pounds of produce, including apples, peaches, and corn, were lost, and all livestock was killed, including the fine racing horses many of the wealthy families owned. Split-rail fences and barns were burned, and slaves were rounded up and marched off. Even though the British army occupied Locust Hill plantation for a while, it did not destroy it.

During this time food became scarce, and catching wild game was a necessity. When he was seven years old, Meriwether was presented with one of his father's hunting rifles, and it was never far out of reach from then on. Since he did not go to school—no children did then—Meriwether had lots of time to roam the foothills of the Blue Ridge Mountains practicing his shooting. Of course he was under strict instructions to run home if he ever saw a British soldier, but for the most part Meriwether rambled in the woods alone.

Sometimes Meriwether would hike through the woods with his mother, watching as she picked wild plants for her herbal remedies. He had a thousand and one questions for her about the plants, animals, fish, and birds they saw. Lucy knew the answer to many of his questions.

Finally in October 1781, the British commander, General Cornwallis, surrendered his army to General George Washington at Yorktown. The colonists were now free. The war was over.

Slowly life on the plantation began to return to "normal." Uncle Nicholas began teaching Meriwether how to run the plantation. Meriwether had many things to learn, and although the eight-year-old boy tried hard to concentrate on everything his uncle told him, his heart longed to be in the hills, hunting for deer and wolves. Out in the wilderness he liked to pretend he was Daniel Boone, who ventured through the Cumberland Gap and into the wild frontier of Kentucky. Meriwether wished for that kind of exciting life.

In 1783 Meriwether's wish came true. His step-father announced they were moving to be part of a new colony on the Broad River in northeastern Georgia. The Locust Hill plantation would be looked after by Nicholas Lewis until Meriwether was old enough to return and run it himself. Meriwether was overjoyed. This was precisely the kind of adventure he had been dreaming of!

All of Meriwether's relatives and many neighbors came to a huge farewell party. Thomas Jefferson was there, too, since his estate, Monticello, was next to Locust Hill. As much as Meriwether hated to say good-bye to people he had known all his life, he was eager to see new sights and experience new adventures.

When the Lewis/Marks family set out on the four-hundred-mile trek to Georgia, they traveled in a caravan that included several other prominent Virginia families who were going to the same place. It was quite a procession that headed out across the gently sloping Piedmont plateau. Sturdy oxen pulled covered wagons, dogs ran in and out between the wheels, and slaves walked alongside leading pigs on short tethers. Meriwether was constantly on the lookout for game, and he shot many deer, wild turkeys, and opossums, which his mother cooked when they made camp each evening.

The caravan skirted the edge of the Appalachian Mountain chain as it made its way through the Carolinas and on into Georgia.

When the travelers finally arrived in Oglethorpe County, Captain Marks selected a homestead site

for the family upstream from most of the other settlers, right on the edge of the forest. Meriwether felt
at home there from the start. The forest was full of
deer and opossums to hunt, as in Virginia, and
there were other animals too, including beavers
and bears. Meriwether was not afraid of any of
them. Even though he was only nine years old, he
soon earned a reputation for being as brave and
clear-thinking in dangerous situations as any
grown man.

As it happened, the family had just planted its
first corn crop when Meriwether's reputation was
put to the test. Dawn was breaking when everyone
inside the Markses' cabin was startled awake by
frantic banging on the door.

"Quickly, let us in and bar the door behind us."
It was their neighbor Mr. Herbert.

Captain Marks jumped up and pulled the cabin
door open. With a rush, nine people tumbled
inside.

"It's Indians!" Mr. Herbert panted. "They
attacked the Atkins' cabin. As far as I know, everyone escaped into the woods. But they're bound to
attack again soon. I figured there was safety in
numbers."

As Mr. Herbert spoke, he took up a position
along the wall of the log cabin, his musket stick-
ing out through one of the holes provided for that
very purpose. Three other neighbors lined up
beside him, the barrels of their muskets glistening
in the early morning sun. The women and girls,
some carrying cooking pots or sacks of food, gathered beside the table.

Meriwether's younger brother Reuben began to whimper. Meriwether could not understand why his brother was scared. He found the situation very exciting. His mind was buzzing with ideas and images as he tried to think of ways to outsmart the Indians and protect everyone inside the cabin. His heart beat wildly when his mother handed him his rifle and he joined the men at the wall.

Everyone waited in silence, their ears attuned to the smallest crackle of a twig or the rustle of a bush outside.

After fifteen minutes of anxious waiting, Captain Marks broke the silence. "This may not be a good idea," he said. "We're sitting like birds on a nest here. If the Indians set the cabin on fire, they'll flush us all out."

"I was beginning to think the same thing. And there's no one to come to our rescue if we do get flushed out," Mr. Herbert said.

"What should we do, then?" Meriwether's mother asked.

"Let's hide in the woods, at least for a day or so. The Indians won't know where to look for us there," Captain Marks replied.

Meriwether's mother pulled the quilts off the beds and dressed Reuben in an extra pair of leather pants and a thick woolen jacket. The rest of the family also put on an extra layer of clothing. Making sure he and Meriwether had a good supply of gunpowder and shot with them, Captain Marks opened the cabin door. Meriwether felt a blast of cold air on his face as he stepped out into the crisp morning air.

"Where do you think we should head?" Captain Marks whispered to Meriwether.

It may have sounded strange for a man to be asking the advice of a nine-year-old boy, but Meriwether knew the forest around the cabin better than anyone else. He had spent hundreds of hours creeping through the trees and brush in search of wildlife and unusual plants.

Meriwether thought for a moment. "If we go left, we'll come to a small clearing surrounded by post oaks. It's a place where the deer gather."

Captain Marks put his hand on his stepson's shoulder. "You lead the way. We are relying on you," he said.

Meriwether slung his rifle over his shoulder and stepped to the front of the group. He had hunted with his dogs in the woods many times at night and knew the woods held nothing to fear except the Indians. Except for Reuben's quiet crying, they walked on in silence until they came to the clearing. Meriwether's mother threw the quilts down on the ground, and everyone huddled together on them. The men sat around the outside of the group, their rifles trained on the surrounding forest.

The day dragged on. Everyone froze at the sound of rustling among the trees, but it turned out to be a wildcat.

At dusk one of the men gathered wood for a fire while another drew water from a nearby creek. Over the fire Mrs. Herbert and her twelve-year-old daughter, Lydia, prepared corn gruel for everyone to eat.

As thin wisps of smoke from the fire spiraled up through the trees, darkness fell over the clearing. With the darkness came the sound of the crackling of twigs in the forest. They all stopped what they were doing and listened anxiously.

"Ay ahhhh!" Meriwether heard the bloodcurdling Indian war cry as gunshots erupted from among the trees. The group in the clearing was thrown into chaos. The women grabbed the children and dragged them into the undergrowth while the men aimed their rifles into the moonless night and fired randomly. Meriwether watched the scene, his senses alert. What should he do? He looked at the fire and the way the men were silhouetted against its orange glow, making them easy targets for the Indians. Someone had to put out that fire. Meriwether sprinted to the cooking area and grabbed a pot of water. With a single action he picked up the pot and threw the water onto the flames. Hiss. The fire died, and it was dark.

"Spread out," Meriwether whispered to the men as he crept toward one of the towering oak trees to take cover.

The group waited through the night, but they heard no more gunshots. To be safe, they stayed in the clearing for one more day before heading back to their cabins. As they dispersed, the men patted Meriwether on the back. "You did a man's job out there last night," they told him.

Deep inside Meriwether knew they were right. Even though he was only nine years old, he was the only one who had had the presence of mind to douse the fire when the Indians attacked. Some-how, when the minds of the others were clouded with panic, his mind had become clearer than ever. It was a trait that would serve Meriwether well in the adventures he would experience later in life.

Chapter 3

Looking for Adventure

When Meriwether Lewis was thirteen, his mother announced it was time for him to return to Virginia so that he could learn how to be a first-rate plantation owner. Meriwether wasn't eager to go. He loved living with his close-knit family, which now included his two-year-old half-brother, John Marks.

Meriwether's sister, Jane, traveled with him, which made the parting a little easier. Now that she was fifteen, it was time for her to be married, and their mother had arranged a match for her with a man who lived in Richmond, Virginia.

In the fall of 1787 Meriwether arrived back at Locust Hill. He had been away with his family in Georgia for four years. When he had left, he had little idea of the amount of land and property he owned. Now it amazed him. He owned land for as far as he could see.

Meriwether discovered that Locust Hill had been well run in his absence. Uncle Nicholas had built up the number of livestock on the plantation, and the fields were yielding a fine harvest of wheat and corn.

Part of becoming a good plantation owner meant getting some formal education. While they were in Georgia, Meriwether's mother had taught him to read and write, but he wanted to know more than that. He wanted to know about mathematics, natural science, and English. His uncle set about finding him a tutor.

Soon Meriwether and his cousin Peachy Gilmer moved in with a tutor named Parson Maury. Parson Maury had a large library, and Meriwether constantly had his nose in a book. He loved reading about the adventures of Captain James Cook, a British sea captain who explored the South Pacific Ocean. In 1768 Cook became the first man to sail around New Zealand, proving that it was two separate islands and not merely a peninsula of Australia. Cook also had with him a botanist named Joseph Banks, who made notes on the flora and fauna he encountered. Meriwether read all about the plants and animals that Banks and Cook had discovered.

During breaks in his education Meriwether went home to Locust Hill to learn more about running the plantation. A plantation was like a small village. Locust Hill had twenty-four slaves, who worked the plantation. Each slave had a specific job to do. Some were blacksmiths who shoed the horses and made the plows; others were carpenters, barrel makers, whiskey distillers, weavers, and shoemakers. Still others worked the fields, planting, weeding, and harvesting the crops. All these people looked to Meriwether, as plantation owner, to provide for their needs.

A good plantation owner was supposed to increase the size of his land holdings by buying more land, and Meriwether was no exception. Under his uncle's guidance he purchased 800 acres of land on the bank of the Red River in Montgomery County to the south and another 180 acres in Clarke County to the north.

In 1790 Meriwether wrote to his mother, "I expect to continue for eighteen months or two years. Every civility is here paid to me and leaves me without any reason to regret the loss of a home of nearer connection. As soon as I complete my education, you shall certainly see me."

As it turned out, Meriwether got to see his mother a lot sooner than he had planned, but under sad circumstances. Captain Marks died, leaving Meriwether's mother with Reuben, John, and another baby, a little girl named Mary, to look after. It was as if history was repeating itself. As Captain Marks's only son, John inherited everything his father had owned. Once again this left Lucy Lewis Marks with no money or land of her own. As soon as he heard about his stepfather's death, Meriwether wrote to his mother right away, inviting her, Reuben, John, and Mary to come to Virginia and live at Locust Hill with him.

In April 1792, Lucy Lewis Marks and her family returned to Locust Hill. Now that she was back, it seemed to Meriwether that her only concern was to find a suitable wife for him. Meriwether was six feet tall by now, with curly brown hair and piercing blue eyes—a fine catch for any southern belle, his mother insisted. But Meriwether did not want to settle down with a family. The truth was, he was bored with the routine of planting and harvesting, spring dances and fall hayrides, and formal dinners at neighboring estates. What he wanted was adventure, and that lay just around the corner—or so he thought.

On May 11, 1792, an American captain named Robert Gray sailed his ship up the Pacific Coast of North America. Reaching the mouth of a large river, he anchored in its estuary. From the width of the river, Gray recognized it to be major waterway. He named it the Columbia River after his ship. Due to recent advances in clock making, Gray carried with him an extremely accurate clock that allowed him to plot exactly where he was on a map. As a result, he was able to fix the latitude and longitude of the mouth of the Columbia River.

Fixing the latitude and longitude in this way meant that other captains could find the exact location of the river mouth anytime they wanted. It also meant that an explorer could set out from the east coast of the North American continent and know exactly in which direction to head overland to reach the mouth of the Columbia River.

This discovery had piqued the interest of Thomas Jefferson, who was serving as the United States' first Secretary of State, and in January 1793 Jefferson made a startling announcement. He was looking for a single brave man who, along with an assistant, would be willing to travel overland to the mouth of the Columbia River. No one knew what the middle of the continent was like, because no white man had ever ventured that far inland. There were rumors of mountains made of solid gold, of huge man-eating dinosaurs roaming the swamps, of savage Indians, and even of a tribe of blond-haired people who spoke Swedish.

This was just the type of adventure Meriwether Lewis had been waiting for. He would be able to hike and explore, meet Indians, and observe strange and unknown plants and animals. He hurried off to apply for the position.

In February Jefferson was going to announce who the first man to cross the American continent to the Pacific Ocean would be. Meriwether waited anxiously. When he found out who the man would be, he could scarcely believe it. Thomas Jefferson had chosen André Michaux, a Frenchman, to be the first person to traverse the American continent. Why hadn't he chosen an American for the job?

The cross-continent expedition got under way in June 1793, and it was not long before Jefferson wished he had selected an American. André

Michaux had traveled only as far as Kentucky when Jefferson learned that he was a secret agent for the French government. Far from investigating what lay in the center of the continent, Michaux's real mission was to raise an army of American men to attack Spanish landowners west of the Mississippi River. Jefferson protested to the French government, which finally ordered Michaux to abandon his mission and return home. Nothing more was said about the expedition, and Meriwether decided that he would have to find some other way to satisfy his quest for adventure.

The next opportunity to escape the boredom of life at Locust Hill came a year later. This time it was not a journey of exploration that caught Meriwether's attention but rather an event called the Whiskey Rebellion.

The new United States government was having a hard time raising enough money to fund itself and all the projects it had promised to carry out, especially industrial expansion in the East. Secretary of the Treasury Alexander Hamilton came up with a way to quickly get more money. The Pennsylvania counties west of the Appalachian Mountains had taken to turning their wheat crop into whiskey, so why not tax the whiskey? There were other taxes in the United States at this time, but they were all taxes on imported products. The whiskey tax was the first tax the new government had placed on something produced within the states.

Of course the wheat growers in the western counties were furious. They asked what they would gct in return for the tax. Did the government intend to protect them from the Indians, who often attacked, or build better roads and canals in the area? No! Instead the government wanted to tax them and spend their hard-earned money to build more factories and warehouses for rich industrialists in the East.

George Washington soon got the message that the farmers were going to stand up and fight for the right not to be taxed. The farmers tarred and feathered some tax collectors and shot others. Homes were burned, and government agents were run out of town.

In August 1794 President Washington called for thirteen thousand volunteers from the East to march across the mountains and quell the Whiskey Rebellion, which was, in fact, America's first civil war.

By now Meriwether's mother and Reuben were quite capable of running Locust Hill without him, so Meriwether became one of the first men to volunteer to fight. He was filled with thoughts of adventure and the vague memory of his father in a soldier's uniform.

Meriwether became Private Lewis of the Virginia Volunteer Corps. Soon he was marching off to invade western Pennsylvania. Since everyone knew he was a wealthy landowner, he was invited into the ranks of the junior officers, although he was only a private.

By the time the troops marched into Pittsburgh, the rebels had fled down the Ohio River and into

Spanish-governed Louisiana. Even so, the rebels had made their point, and the government dropped the idea of a whiskey tax.

With the rebellion over, it was time for the men to march home again, but Private Meriwether Lewis was reluctant to return to the quiet life at Locust Hill. He joined a small military contingent that was staying behind in Pittsburgh to keep the peace and make sure the rebellion did not flare up again. On November 24, 1794, he wrote home to his mother: "I am situated on the Mongahale [Monongahela], about 15 miles above Pittsburgh where we shall be forted this winter…I am in perfect health. I am quite delighted with the soldier's life." He ended his letter by saying, "I would wish Rubin to amuse himself with ucefull books. If he will pay attention he may be adiquate to the task the ensuing year."

The task Meriwether was referring to was running Locust Hill. The spelling in his letter was no better or worse than anyone else's spelling at the time. Since there was no standard dictionary, people felt free to spell words, even their own names or the names of family members, in a variety of ways.

By Christmas the dreary work of supervising the building of army huts had begun to depress Meriwether, who wrote to his mother again: "I am a more confined overseer here than when I was at Locust Hill, having been ever since my last [letter] constantly confined to the huting department. There is no probability of a cessation of axes untill the middle of next month."

Despite the tedium of the work, Meriwether did not consider returning to Locust Hill. Instead he lived in the hope that another exciting episode in his military career lay just ahead.

When his tour of duty at Pittsburgh was finally over, Meriwether signed up again, this time to protect the small villages and isolated farms along the western frontier from Indian attack. He was promoted to the rank of officer under General Wayne, whose nickname was Mad Wayne.

Not long after enlisting, Meriwether got into a political argument with Lieutenant Elliot, one of the other officers in his company. To defend his honor, Meriwether challenged Lieutenant Elliot to a duel at sunrise the next morning, even though duels were now illegal.

Lieutenant Elliot reported the matter to his superior officer, and Meriwether was arrested. At his court martial he pleaded not guilty, though all the evidence said otherwise. However, General Wayne was from the old school of fighting. He encouraged his men to fight duels rather than take matters up in military courts. He insisted that a duel was much cheaper and tended to end an argument permanently.

Meriwether should have been given a dishonorable discharge. Instead he was transferred to the Chosen Rifle Company, a hand-selected group of marksmen. William Clark, a tall, slender man with red hair and a ready smile, was captain of the company, and he and Meriwether soon learned they had many friends and acquaintances in common. Although William was four years older than Meriwether and had been raised near Louisville, Kentucky, members of his family owned land around Charlottesville, Virginia. He was the ninth of ten children, and five of his older brothers, including the famous General George Rogers Clark, had fought in the Revolutionary War. General Clark was also a good friend of Thomas Jefferson.

Meriwether spent an enjoyable year and a half serving under William Clark, and he was sad when William was forced to resign from the army because of family responsibilities. The two men promised to keep in contact by letter.

About the same time that William left the army to return home, Meriwether's mother began a new campaign to try to get her oldest son to return home and settle down. Her campaign did not work. Meriwether was enjoying himself too much out on the western frontier.

One of Meriwether's main jobs was carrying dispatches from one army post to another. This important job required courage and shrewdness as he slipped unnoticed through Indian territory. Meriwether loved the challenge of it all.

Finally, in January 1797, nearly three years after leaving Locust Hill, Meriwether decided he really should go home for a visit. Just as he expected, his mother and Reuben were doing a fine job running the plantation.

Lucy Lewis Marks kept dropping hints to her oldest son about his staying home and taking up his rightful place among Virginia's aristocracy. However, Meriwether could not settle. The West beckoned him in a way he could not fully communicate.

In March 1799 Congress established the new position of regimental paymaster. The officer who was to fill this post needed to be scrupulously honest, since he would be handling large sums of money. He also needed to be punctual because he would be expected to deliver the soldiers' pay on time, no matter what obstacles he encountered along the way.

Meriwether Lewis knew this was the job he wanted, and much to his delight, he was appointed to the position. As regimental paymaster he learned how to handle a boat on the Ohio River, and he galloped through vast tracts of wilderness carrying thousands of dollars in banknotes in his saddlebags. He also carried important news to people living on the frontier. Perhaps the saddest news he had to deliver was that of the death of George Washington, who died just before Christmas 1799. The whole country mourned his passing.

Meriwether's superiors were impressed with the efficient way he did his job, and on December 5, 1800, he was promoted to the rank of captain. Two months later Thomas Jefferson was elected to be the third president of the United States.

Meriwether was not surprised that his old friend had been elected. The country needed a man like Thomas Jefferson at the helm. Jefferson had a way of bringing people together and helping them see what the new nation could become. What Meriwether did not know was that part of Jefferson's vision for the country involved him!

On March 7, 1801, the day after Thomas Jefferson was inaugurated as president, Meriwether received a letter bearing an official government seal. He sat down at his desk and began to read:

"The appointment to the Presidency has rendered it necessary for me to have a private secretary and in selecting one I have thought it important to respect not only his capacity to aid me in the private concerns of the household, but also to contribute to the mass of information which it is interesting to the Administration to acquire. Your knowledge of the Western Country, of the Army, and of all its interests and relations has rendered it desirable for public as well as private purposes that you should be engaged in that office."

Meriwether paused for a moment to take in what he was reading. The president of the United States was asking him to be his private secretary.

He read on: "In point of profit it has little to offer; the salary being only 500 D [dollars], which would scarcely be more than an equivalent for your pay and rations, which you would be obliged to relinquish while withdrawn from active service, but retaining your rank and right to rise.... You would, of course, save also the expense of subsistence and lodgings, as you would be one of my family."

Once again Meriwether stopped and took a deep breath. He really was being asked to come to the new capital city of Washington and live in the president's house.

It was an astonishing offer, one that Meriwether Lewis knew he wanted. He wrote back to Jefferson immediately, agreeing to take up the new post. He then asked the quartermaster for two packhorses. It was time to load up his belongings and head back east.

Chapter 4

Terra Incognita

Twenty-seven-year-old Captain Meriwether Lewis rode into Washington on April 1, 1801, an overladen packhorse in tow. A second packhorse had gone lame and had been left at an army post along the way. Although it was only 250 miles from Pittsburgh to Washington, it had taken Meriwether twenty-two days to complete the journey. Torrential rain, mudslides, and the lame horse had all slowed him down.

Meriwether was eager to see all there was of the new capital. It was only six months ago that the government had moved from Philadelphia to Washington. Many people, though, called it "Wilderness City," since it appeared to have been built in the middle of nowhere. Meriwether was well aware that Washington was not a well-respected town. In fact, it was the laughingstock of many European visitors. As he rode down Pennsylvania Avenue, Meriwether could understand why. The roads were unpaved, and the president's house was a square building that looked more like a plantation house than a residence befitting the leader of a growing country.

When Meriwether arrived at the president's house, he was met by a servant who informed him that Jefferson was visiting Monticello. Meriwether stayed the night in Washington, and the next morning he headed out for Albemarle County to greet his new employer at his estate. At Monticello Meriwether smiled to himself as he bowed to the president. Jefferson was still wearing the same old carpet slippers he always wore. Fame had obviously not changed his unassuming ways.

Once he had settled in at Monticello, Meriwether rode over to Locust Hill. Again he found everyone was well. Reuben was thriving in his role as plantation manager.

Three weeks later President Jefferson and Meriwether Lewis returned to Washington. As the two men entered the president's house, they were met by one of the eleven servants who had moved to Washington from Monticello. Meriwether watched as the servant's face lit up. Thomas Jefferson seemed to have that effect on just about everyone he met, whether a black slave or a famous scientist. People liked to be around him, and Meriwether knew the next four years were going to be very enjoyable.

"The place has twenty-three rooms," Jefferson grumbled to Meriwether as they walked inside, "and not one of them is finished. The roof leaks, the walls haven't been plastered, and there's not even a sta ble. I need more money from Congress to finish the place, but it's not an easy job getting them to part with money. We're lucky it's springtime. Mrs. Adams tells me she nearly froze in here over the winter."

"I can imagine," Meriwether exclaimed as he studied the high ceilings and the gray unfinished walls of the president's house.

"Still, we have to make the most of it," Jefferson smiled. "I've put you in the East Room. That's where Mrs. Adams used to hang her laundry, you know. It's not finished yet, but I had the lines taken down, and it's not in any worse shape than the rest of this monstrosity. We'll be like two mice in a church here, just you and I."

"Yes, we will," Meriwether replied, recalling how he had been nine years old when President Jefferson's wife, Martha, died. The president had two daughters, Patsy and Molly, but they were both married and had children of their own. So apart from the servants, Meriwether would be living there alone with the president.

Jefferson pointed to a wooden door off to the left. "That's your room. I'll see you in my office when you have had a chance to put your things away. That's my office over there." He pointed to a door farther along on the other side of the hall.

Meriwether bowed to the president and then opened the door into his new quarters. Light flooded into the huge room from a row of tall windows. The room was furnished very simply with a

bed, side table, wardrobe, bookshelf, and desk—
all the furniture Meriwether needed. Meriwether
laid his coat and hat on the bed, knowing that one
of the servants would put them away for him. He
stepped over to the side table, poured some water
from the large jug into a white porcelain bowl, and
with both hands splashed cold water onto his
face.

Feeling refreshed, he made his way to the president's office. The office was not finished yet either,
but the rows of neatly stacked books in the book-
cases that lined the unfinished walls made the
room feel somehow cheery and comfortable and
welcoming.

"Ah, Meriwether," the president said, looking up
from a document he was reading. "Sit down, and I
will explain what needs to be done first."

"Yes, sir," Meriwether said as he sank into a
comfortable leather chair. Right then a mocking-
bird on a perch began to squawk. "Pay him no
mind," Jefferson said. "He has something to say
about everything. Smart bird, though. I'm training
him to climb stairs."

Meriwether chuckled. Who would have thought
the president of the United States would take the
time to befriend a bird? But that was exactly the
type of man Thomas Jefferson was. He was interested even in little things like birds.

"Now look here," the president said, spreading a
document on the desk between them. "This is a list
of every commissioned officer in the United States
army."

Meriwether glanced down the first page, which contained many names that he recognized.

"As you know, one of the promises the Democratic-Republicans made was to cut the size of the army in half. It costs far too much money to run, and there is no need for so many men in service now that France does not appear to be ready to declare war on the United States over the Indian troubles and relations with the British have settled down."

Meriwether nodded.

Jefferson continued. "I have devised a code with eleven symbols. I need you to evaluate every commissioned officer on the list and put a symbol beside each name. This is how it works. We start at the top. The three crosses are for officers who are first-class. They must be well respected by their men, have an excellent understanding of military strategy, and be physically ready to command at a moment's notice. At the bottom of the list are those men with three minuses. They are the ones who have no place being in the army. These officers were probably appointed solely because they or their family gave large sums of money to the Federalists, but they have no business commanding men in the United States army."

"I can think of a few names in that category already," Meriwether replied. Now he understood why Jefferson had asked him to be his private secretary. Probably more than any other single person, Meriwether Lewis knew about the officers in the army. He not only had spent time with many of them but also had spent time with the men under their command. He knew which officers were well respected and which were despised because they were lazy or were drunk most of the time.

Jefferson flicked through the many pages in front of him. "This is going to take you a while," he said. "When you are finished, I will use the information to let half the officers go. But I need to be sure I am keeping my best men."

Meriwether nodded. He had an important job ahead of him, and he intended to do it in the fairest manner possible. He was about to make or break the careers of many officers with the stroke of his pen.

Meriwether worked on the list until it was finished. Then the president asked him to draw up a list of all United States postmasters, including the exact location of their post offices and how much money each one was paid.

Along with these tasks, Meriwether copied out Jefferson's first State of the Union address to Congress. The president did not want to give the speech himself. He was well aware that he had a squeaky voice and no one particularly enjoyed listening to him speak to large crowds. Still, Meriwether was surprised when Jefferson asked him to deliver the speech to Congress. Since both George Washington and John Adams had enjoyed giving their own speeches, it marked the first time that anyone other than the president had given the State of the Union speech. Meriwether wrote home to tell his mother about the event. He was sure it was something she would want to tell the neighbors about.

Because of his position as the president's private secretary, there was probably no one else in the entire United States who got to meet as many interesting people as did Meriwether Lewis. And he loved every minute of it. At Jefferson's dinner parties, Meriwether discussed poetry with Philip Freneau and quizzed Thomas Paine, recently returned to the United States, on his escapades in England and France. He listened as a sea captain explained the latest instruments used in navigation and a botanist described the new Linnaeus system for classifying plants.

Sometimes the conversation at these events turned to the great, mysterious expanse of land west of the Mississippi River known as Louisiana. Though Native American tribes had inhabited this land for many thousands of years, they did not have access to large quantities of weapons and were not unified enough to fend off invaders. Many countries had their eye on this huge tract of land, but no one had a definite hold on it. The British planned to colonize southward from Canada; the Spanish had plans to spread north from their territories in Texas and east from California; the French were slowly building forts up the Mississippi from the port of New Orleans; even the Russians had thoughts of moving southward from Alaska. As well, small farmers in the United States were always scheming ways to move across the Mississippi River into the fertile plains rumored to be to the west.

But were there fertile plains there at all? No one knew for sure what was out there beyond the reach of "civilization." On maps the territory of Louisiana was listed as Terra Incognita, or unknown land or country.

Jefferson often spent evenings poring over maps and books, trying to catch a glimpse of what lay beyond the western boundary of the United States. He came to some startling conclusions, none of which Meriwether or any of the educated men who came to dinner had reason to doubt. Jefferson often told Meriwether he believed the Blue Ridge Mountains were the highest on the continent. It was common knowledge that there were mountains on the western edge of the continent— Captain Cook had noted them on his voyage up the coast. But no one could imagine mountains higher than what had already been seen in the East. The president was also optimistic about finding woolly mammoths and other prehistoric animals out in the middle of the continent. And why not? There were also rumors of mountains made of pure salt and erupting volcanoes.

Several weeks later a book arrived that answered some of these questions and raised many others. The book was titled *Voyages from Montreal, on the River St. Lawrence, Through the Continent of North America, to the Frozen and Pacific Ocean* and was by a man named Alexander Mackenzie.

As Meriwether entered Jefferson's office the day the book arrived, the president jumped to his feet and announced enthusiastically, "Mackenzie's book is here at last. It's taken him nine years to get it published, but finally it's done." He held the book up for Meriwether to see. Meriwether could feel his pulse quicken as he fixed his eyes on the book.

"What a treasure trove," Jefferson went on. "I haven't been able to put it down since it arrived this morning. Listen to this! 'In compliance with the chief's request I desired my people to take their bundles, and lay them down on the bank of the river. In the mean time I went to take the dimensions of his large canoe, in which, it was signified to me, that about ten winters ago he went a considerable distance towards the mid-day sun, with forty of his people, when he saw two large vessels full of such men as myself, by whom he was kindly received: they were, he said, the first white people he had seen. They were probably the ships commanded by Captain Cook.' Can you imagine that? An Indian chief who saw both Captain Cook and Alexander Mackenzie!"

Meriwether leaned over to look at the passage for himself. It was amazing. He already knew that Alexander Mackenzie was a fur trapper who commanded Fort Chipewyan, on Lake Athabasca, a trading post for the British-owned North West Company. Mackenzie had longed to find a northwest passage across the continent and claim it for Great Britain. His first attempt to find it, in 1789, had led him much farther north than he had intended, and he had arrived at the north coast of Canada, reaching the Arctic and not the Pacific Ocean. Four years later, in 1793, he tried again. This time he followed a more southerly route from Lake Athabasca, and in July he reached the Pacific

Ocean near the northern end of Vancouver Island. In doing so, Alexander Mackenzie became the first European to reach the Pacific Coast north of Mexico by traveling overland from the East. It had taken him nine years to publish his journal because he had been so disappointed at not being able to find a river route suitable for crossing the continent. Although he had crossed the Rocky Mountains on foot, he was now sure that an exploration party would have to go farther south to find a more passable route across them. Knowing all of this was one thing, but reading Alexander Mackenzie's own account of events was quite another.

Jefferson flipped to the back of the book and began reading another passage. "'Now I mixed up some vermillion in melted grease, and inscribed, in large characters, on the south-east face of the rock on which we had slept last night, this brief memorial—"Alexander Mackenzie, from Canada, by land, the twenty-second of July, one thousand seven hundred and ninety-three."'"

"That was nine years ago! And what has the United States done about it? Other than the André Michaux debacle, we haven't made a serious attempt to find a river passage to the Pacific Ocean. Mark my words. If we don't do something soon, the British will secure the entire west coast of the continent. We must do something to stop them!" the president said.

Meriwether looked into Thomas Jefferson's hazel eyes, which were ablaze with determination.

"We can't wait any longer," Jefferson went on. "We have to beat the British in finding a practical route west. Whoever finds it first will have a way to trade with China and get into the lucrative sea otter trade Captain Cook wrote about. Besides, if I have anything to do with it, one day the United States will stretch from the Atlantic all the way to the Pacific. I hope the day comes when the entire continent will be populated by people speaking one language, governed in similar forms and by similar laws. Anything short of that will represent a failure to develop the influence our nation can have on all that surrounds her. We must establish an American route across the center of the continent, over the Rocky Mountains, and down the Columbia River. Alexander Mackenzie and his British sponsors are not going to get their way!"

"But what about the mountains?" Meriwether asked. "How impenetrable are they?"

"That's just it—they shouldn't be very difficult," the president replied. "Mackenzie says in his journal that he and his men carried the boats over the mountains in just one day. It's only about four or five hundred miles south of there where an American would cross them. Surely the mountains must be of similar height and width in both places."

"One day's portage," Meriwether exclaimed. "Why, that might be the simplest part of the entire trip!"

Throughout the rest of the hot afternoon, Thomas Jefferson and Meriwether Lewis huddled over Alexander Mackenzie's journal, comparing entries in it with Antoine Soulard's newly released map of the North American continent. By early evening the two men had devised a plan—an expedition to cross the American continent to the Pacific Ocean.

Both men agreed that the most direct route across the continent would be to travel up the Missouri River to its source, which was assumed— but not proven—to be in the Rocky Mountains. This would be followed by a one-day portage over the mountains to the headwaters of the Columbia River on the other side. Several sea captains, such as James Cook and George Vancouver, as well as Robert Gray, had plotted the mouth of the Columbia River, though no one knew where it began. However, Jefferson and Meriwether both thought that an expedition following this route would not have too much difficulty finding the headwaters of the river once it was actually in the area.

Once the route had been worked out, the two men turned their attention to what such an expedition should accomplish.

"Just think of the information that could be gathered along the way!" the president exclaimed, reaching for his quill pen. He dipped the pen into the inkwell on his desk and wrote on a sheet of paper, "Advantages of such an Expedition." Under that title he wrote, "Diplomatic ties with the Indian Tribes along the way."

"Think of it, Meriwether," he said, looking up from the paper and mopping the sweat from his brow, "the opportunities it would provide for the United States to entice the Indians to trade with us and not the French or the British. It would give the

United States the potential to be the biggest fur trader in the world. Ha! I wonder how the British would take that?"

"And look at the map," Meriwether said, pointing at Soulard's map. "There are still huge tracts of land labeled 'Unknown Country.' Who knows what waterways lie in those unknown places?"

Jefferson added "New Waterways" to the list. By the time supper was ready, the list had many other items, including "Drawing up accurate maps," "Studying the plants, animals, landforms, minerals, and soils along the way," and "Counting the number of Indian Tribes, noting their relationships with each other, the food they ate, what they wear, where they live, and their social customs."

"Quite a list!" Jefferson remarked as the two men made their way to the dining room for supper. "I hope I can find a man who can accomplish it all. No doubt the man who leads this expedition will have to be a scientist."

Later that night Meriwether lay awake in bed. An owl hooted loudly outside his window, and he could hear dogs barking in the distance. But they were not keeping him awake—his thoughts were. One moment he imagined himself setting out on the expedition, gun in hand, leading twenty or forty or even one hundred men into the unknown areas of the American continent. The next moment the words of the president echoed in his ears: "No doubt the man who leads this expedition will have to be a scientist." Meriwether could hardly claim to be in that category.

The question was, did he have any chance of leading such an expedition? One moment Meriwether was hopeful, the next he felt deflated. He tossed and turned until the morning light filtered in through the blue silk drapes. As he splashed cold water on his face that morning, Meriwether made a decision. He would not ask the president to consider him to lead the expedition. No, he would continue to help with the planning and see what happened next.

Chapter 5

Planning

At breakfast Jefferson and Meriwether continued planning. The more they talked, the longer the list grew of the things the expedition could discover. Finally the president broached the subject of an expedition leader. "And what kind of man do you think we should be looking for to lead such an expedition?" he asked Meriwether.

Gulping hard, determined not to let the president see how desperately he wanted the job himself, Meriwether said, "I think he would have to be a man trained to lead men, and he would need to know a lot about the West, as far as that is possible."

"I agree," Jefferson interjected. "But if we need him to observe and record all this information along the way, he would have to be a scientist. And that's where I'm torn. What would be better, an ornithologist, a mineralogist, or a botanist? What do you think?"

"It is hard to say," Meriwether replied, aware of how lame he sounded. "We really need someone who is all three and who knows enough about astronomy to take accurate readings from the stars."

"And that precisely is the problem I have been turning about in my head all night. I don't think there is such an individual in the United States, or anywhere," the president said. "I have come to the conclusion that I shall have to select a man who has some of these qualities, the ones that cannot be taught, like good leadership skills and my complete trust, and then I shall have to have him educated in the areas where he lacks knowledge."

"In that case you will have to find someone who is a quick learner, since you hope to launch the expedition within the year," Meriwether pointed out.

"Quite right," Jefferson said, reaching out and clapping Meriwether on the shoulder. "In that case I consider it settled. We begin your education tomorrow!"

Meriwether stared at the president. Had he heard right? Did Thomas Jefferson really mean that he would be the leader of the expedition? And if so, was he up to the task of learning all that Jefferson thought he should know for the trip? It had all seemed so simple as he lay in bed last night. But now that the opportunity appeared to have presented itself, Meriwether was awash with doubt about leading the expedition.

"Do you mean that you want me to lead the party?" he spluttered, knowing he sounded stupid.

"I do indeed!" Jefferson laughed. "You possess the qualities one man cannot teach another. By all accounts you are fair with the men under your command, there was never any question of your honesty when you were regimental paymaster, and you showed undaunted courage when you were required to slip through enemy lines to deliver dispatches. Furthermore, I have observed you with many of my dinner guests, and while you may not have been to university, I consider you to have the intellect to comprehend scientific principles and practices when they are explained to you. And above all, you have my complete and utter confidence. I knew your father long before you were born, and I know you to be of the same fine character as he was."

Meriwether felt tears welling in his eyes. Although he tried desperately not to let them spill onto his cheeks, they did anyway. It was an honor for him to be selected to lead the expedition, and just as much an honor to be likened to the father he barely remembered.

Later that day Meriwether slipped outside and sat quietly, thinking of the enormous task that lay ahead of him. He wondered whether it was really possible for anyone to fulfill all of the expectations President Jefferson had for this unique trip. Could he learn enough to make useful identifications of

uncategorized plants and animals and to understand the ways of the Indians he met? He would be
meeting warriors from powerful tribes. Would he be
able to convince them that he was friendly and
that he represented a country on the East Coast of
the continent that wanted to make alliances with
them? It seemed a tall order, since they would have
no common language. But one thing he had no
doubt about. He knew he would get to the West
Coast or die trying.

Jefferson and Meriwether talked of little else in
the days that followed. They met together each day
to discuss the details of the trip. Often the president would pace the floor, stopping from time to
time to admire the new garden that lay beyond the
open window. The colors of the flowers were vibrant
in the midsummer sunlight.

"How many men do you think should go on the
expedition?" Jefferson asked one afternoon.

It was a good question. Meriwether and Jefferson had agreed that each man on the expedition
should be young, unmarried, fit, and have a specific skill. They needed men who were hunters,
boatmen, blacksmiths, and cooks. They also needed
men who could tan animal hides and sew them
into boots, clothing, and packs. The problem was
that although they knew the kind of men they
wanted for the trip, they had no idea how many of
them they needed.

"At first I thought perhaps thirty or even forty
men," Jefferson continued before Meriwether could
form an answer to the question. "But it would cost

a lot of money to outfit and feed them all. I doubt Congress would be very willing to allocate a large sum of money just so a group of men can go and explore land that doesn't even belong to the United States."

"Yes," Meriwether replied, "and then you have to worry that a large group of white men heading into the wilderness might alarm the Indian chiefs along the way. They might well think it was a small army sent out to subdue their tribe."

"Hmmm," the president pondered, "but on the other hand, a small party has its own problems. If we send only seven or eight men on the expedition, how will they protect themselves if they are attacked? And what would happen if a sickness spread through the camp? If half the men died of illness, that would leave only three or four men to carry on. Besides, some jobs are so important that two men who know how to do them are needed so that one can act as a backup for the other."

"Perhaps we should meet halfway and take twelve to fifteen men on the expedition," Meriwether suggested.

"Yes, I think that could work," Jefferson said, and then changing the subject he said, "Let's go over the route again."

Meriwether and the president pored over Antoine Soulard's map of North America. Eventually they decided that Meriwether and his team, whom Jefferson thought should be called the Corps of Discovery, should assemble in Pittsburgh and then travel by boat down the Ohio River to the

Mississippi and then up the Mississippi to the mouth of the Missouri River. The town of St. Louis was located at the confluence of the Mississippi and Missouri Rivers, and it would be the last major town the expedition would pass through. From there the expedition would follow the basic route the men had agreed upon earlier: up the Missouri River as far as they could go and then over the Rocky Mountains to the Columbia River, carrying their boat. From there they would float down the river until they reached the Pacific Ocean. Once they had reached the ocean, they would locate a fur trading ship and have it take them down the west coast of the American continents, around Cape Horn, and up the east coast to the West Indies. Once they reached these islands, they would find another ship headed for Philadelphia.

It would be a long trip. Since Robert Gray had fixed the location of the mouth of the Columbia River at 124 degrees longitude and 46 degrees latitude, Jefferson was able to work out that the North American continent was roughly three thousand miles across. The trip back from the West Coast by ship would be at least three times that distance.

Because of the distance, the plan called for the expedition to stop somewhere along the Missouri River and set up a winter camp. Yet even with this delay, Jefferson estimated that the entire trip would take no more than eighteen months.

Jefferson soon began giving Meriwether botany lessons. An interest in botany was something the two men had in common. Meriwether had been introduced to plants by his mother, who still had a reputation for being able to heal just about any ailment with the right combination of herbs. Because of this interest in plants, Meriwether enjoyed the challenge of raising better crops at Locust Hill. Jefferson confided in Meriwether that botany was his favorite branch of science because of the many wonderful uses of plants. They produced not only food but also herbs for medicines, and the beauty, fragrance, and color of flowers could lift the most downcast heart.

By early September, the plan for the expedition was firmly in place, though they agreed no one else should know about it yet. The president still had to work out the best way to present to Congress the need for money for the Corps of Discovery. It was a delicate matter, since Congress was more interested in spending money in the United States than on exploring foreign lands. If they did not set aside money for the expedition, it would have to be canceled.

And then there was the question of exactly how much it would all cost. Jefferson left Meriwether to figure that out. After breakfast one morning, Meriwether sat down at his desk and pulled several sheets of paper from a drawer. He dipped his quill pen into the ink and began to write a heading on each sheet. On the first he wrote "Items to Trade with Indians." On other sheets he wrote Clothing, Housing, Transportation, Food, Navigational Instruments, Arms, Medicines, Tools, and Miscellaneous. When he was finished, he sat for a moment, letting the enormity of the task sink in. If he forgot something important or ran out of an item before the expedition was over, there would be no way to replace it. He dipped his pen again and began to fill in the first sheet.

The matter of what to take to trade with the Indians was serious. It could perhaps be the difference between life and death because there was no way the party could carry enough food with them for eighteen months. They would have to get food along the way by trading with the local Indians. If the Indians weren't tempted by the items they had to trade, the men on the expedition could starve to death. Meriwether had learned from trappers the kinds of things the Indians as far west as the Mandan would probably want to trade. But what about the tribes west of the Mandan Indians? Would they value the same objects? Was there something else that would be of more value to them? Meriwether had no idea and no way to find out until he saw these Indians face-to-face. Eventually he wrote down beads (blue, orange, yellow, and red), tobacco, brass and iron wire, tomahawks, scalping knives, gunpowder, sewing needles, awls and thimbles, ribbon, muslin, calico, silk, eyeglasses, fish spears, fishhooks, copper kettles, rings, earrings, brooches, bells, scissors, and looking glasses.

By evening Meriwether was still hard at work on his lists. Even with twenty pages of notes, he had barely begun to write down all of the supplies that he would need to buy. By then he was starting to think it would take him years just to gather the materials needed for the trip.

A few days later Meriwether and the president were eating breakfast together again. "How is the planning for the expedition coming along?" Jefferson asked.

"It's a huge task," Meriwether replied. "I have started to make lists of the supplies we will need, but the lists keep growing, and I am anxious to begin purchasing items."

Jefferson laid his hand on Meriwether's shoulder. "I wish you could too. There are so many things that need to be done, but all we can do is plan until the secret is out and Congress approves the money."

"When do you think that will be?" Meriwether questioned.

"It all depends on how the Monroe Project goes," the president sighed. "I am sure we are doing the right thing, but ten million dollars is a vast amount of money to ask Congress to spend. I can count on Democratic-Republicans' votes of course, but some of the Federalists are spoiling for a fight with France and might not want to buy land they could go to war over. It's quite a problem getting the bill passed, as you can imagine."

Meriwether could imagine. The Monroe Project was the most ambitious project President Jefferson had thought up so far. It involved buying New Orleans from the French. It was a complicated arrangement, since the French were not actually present in New Orleans and the port city was still under the control of the Spanish. However, the Spanish had sold the whole of Louisiana to the French two years before. No one in the United States government had been particularly worried about having the Spanish for neighbors. After all, Spain was weak and poor, and the Spanish posed no threat of invading the United States. France, on the other hand, was a different story. French ruler Napoleon Bonaparte was a leader with a thirst for war and for conquering other countries.

Jefferson was sure that the arrival of the French in New Orleans would mean disaster for American farmers west of the Appalachian Mountains because the Spanish, under French influence, had already taken away their right of deposit. This meant that the farmers were not allowed to unload their produce at the docks in New Orleans, where it could be loaded onto ships bound for other countries.

The French had not taken direct control of the vast tract of land they now owned in North America because Napoleon had more important concerns right then. His troops were fighting to regain control of the island of Santo Domingo (Hispaniola) in the Caribbean. The western half of the island had been a French colony until 1800, when a black slave led a successful revolt to free the colony. Napoleon was humiliated at being upstaged by a black revolutionary, and he planned to retaliate by establishing an even larger French colony on Santo Domingo. The ex-slaves banded together to defeat the French invaders, who were themselves dying in huge numbers from yellow fever.

Sensing that Napoleon might be in a mood to review his plans for Louisiana, Jefferson wanted to dispatch James Monroe and Robert Livingston to France to see if they could persuade Napoleon to sell them New Orleans.

This whole concept of buying territory rather than going to war over it was entirely new, and no one was sure whether the French would laugh at it or take it seriously.

Jefferson was pushing Congress to authorize Monroe and Livingston to offer the French up to ten million dollars to seal the deal, which would also include buying parts of Florida if possible. No one really knew how much of Florida the French owned, and it was unlikely the French themselves knew. Such complicated land deals had taken place among the French, Spanish, and British over Florida that no one was sure who owned what parts of the place anymore.

The president had explained to Meriwether that although ten million dollars was a huge sum of money, it made sense to buy the city, since getting into a war with France over the port would in the end cost the United States many times that amount.

"I hope we can avoid war," Jefferson said, glancing at his pocket watch. "It's time for my weekly review with Vice President Burr. I hate to think what he's been up to this time. If ever a man was a bane to me, it is he."

As Jefferson reached the door, he stopped and turned around. "By the way, did I tell you I have applied to the French consulate for a passport so you can travel through Louisiana, and also to the British consulate so you can go through Oregon country. I hope to hear back soon," he said.

"Thank you," Meriwether said. "I'll keep working on the cost estimates."

It took Meriwether several more weeks before he felt reasonably confident that he had listed most of the supplies the Corps of Discovery would need and had worked out how much each item would cost. In the end his list read:

$696 for gifts for the Indians.
$430 for boat and other means of transport.
$217 for mathematical instruments for fixing locations and measuring heights of mountains.
$81 for arms, guns, ball and powder for protection and to shoot wild game.
$225 for camping equipment.
$55 medicines.
$224 food for the trip.
$55 to get the packs made.
$300 to pay hunters, guides, and interpreters.
$100 to take care of the party until they begin the journey.
$81 for emergencies of one type or another.

All in all Meriwether estimated the cost of the expedition to be $2,500.

On January 12, 1803, the United States Congress approved the Monroe Project, and Monroe

and Livingston were dispatched to France. With
that matter out of the way, the president called a
secret meeting of Congress on January 18. At it he
explained the expedition to them for the first time.
He went over Meriwether's planning so far and
pointed out how much money the United States
would be able to make if it could secure the fur
trade from the middle of the continent to the West
Coast and then over the Pacific Ocean to Asia.
When it was put in such terms, Congress had no
problem passing the bill. Indeed, the prospect of
making money for the nation made them very
happy. Meriwether was relieved. Now, for the first
time, he was sure the expedition would go ahead,
and he carried on with his planning with renewed
urgency.

Chapter 6

The Vastness of the Task Before Him

January 18, 1803, the day the bill authorizing the expedition was passed, was a Tuesday. By the following Friday, Meriwether Lewis was sitting in the office of Treasury Secretary Albert Gallatin, who was also a well-respected mapmaker. Meriwether had been at many dinner parties with the treasury secretary, but this was the first time they had discussed the upcoming expedition. The trip had been a secret until the bill authorizing it passed. And even now, only Jefferson's cabinet and members of Congress knew about the plans for the trip.

Gallatin's eyes shone with excitement as he talked to Meriwether. "What an opportunity this is!" he said. "I only wish I were younger. I would come along with you myself."

Meriwether laughed. "You're not the first person to say that to me!"

"And think what it will do for the United States," the treasury secretary continued. "You must concentrate on the country around the Missouri River. I'm quite convinced it will be the next large tract of land lying outside the boundaries of the Union where people from the United States will settle. We must know as much about it as we can. Make sketches of the trees, assess the annual rainfall, take temperature readings, and bring back as many plant and animal specimens as you can, preferably alive." He glanced at Meriwether. "But that's not what the president sent you to talk to me about, is it? What is it he wants from me?"

Meriwether smiled. He was quickly getting used to listening to the special instructions and plans everyone seemed to have for the Corps of Discovery. It was going to be difficult to achieve half of what people had in mind for the expedition.

"President Jefferson has urged me to take careful observations of latitude and longitude at all of the remarkable points along the Missouri River and westward," Meriwether began. "He wants me to pay special attention to river mouths, rapids, islands, and other natural markings. And I am to record all my observations on a birch paper map, since it is less likely to be spoiled if it gets damp."

"Definitely the best paper for the job," Gallatin said. "I think the best thing would be for me to have a map made for you that shows all we know about the land from the Mississippi River west to the Pacific Coast. As I'm sure you're aware, there are only three points on the map that are fixed by latitude and longitude. They are St. Louis, the Mandan villages, and the mouth of the Columbia River. You see how important your work will be! You can fill in the blank spaces on the map as you go, plotting longitude and latitude."

"I'll do my best, sir," Meriwether replied.

An hour later, after Meriwether had thanked Gallatin for his help, the words "you can fill in the blank spaces as you go" were still echoing in his head. No one had any idea of the variety of landforms, climate, and rivers that awaited the expedition west of St. Louis. For a moment Meriwether found himself stunned by the vastness of the task before him.

With the mapmaking process under way, Meriwether turned his attention to the matter of transportation. He intended to go as far as he could by boat and then trade with the Indians for horses when the river ran out. But what kind of boat should he use? He discussed the question many times with Jefferson, and eventually they agreed on a solution. The expedition would use a large keelboat to take them as far up the Missouri River as possible. From there they would use canoes to take them to the headwaters of the river. Then they would need a different sort of boat altogether to carry overland to the headwaters of the Columbia River. This vessel would be a large, collapsible, iron-framed canoe that could be bolted together and covered with animal skins. This would provide them a large, sturdy canoe. And if necessary, it could be taken apart and reassembled many times. There was only one problem: No such boat existed, and so Meriwether set out to design one.

Meriwether conducted many experiments to determine the best shape for the canoe. By late February he was proud to tell Jefferson that he had designed an iron frame that would weigh only forty-four pounds, and once covered with animal hides, it would be capable of carrying over fifteen hundred pounds of cargo.

Jefferson immediately gave Meriwether permission to write to a boat builder in Harpers Ferry with the plans and instructions that he should begin work on the boat at once. If questions were raised, Meriwether was instructed to tell people that he was taking a trip down the Mississippi River, since the true nature of the journey was still a well-kept secret.

By March 16 Meriwether was on his way to Harpers Ferry for a weeklong stay. His plan was to check on the progress of the iron-frame canoe and to order arms and ammunition from the armory for the trip. Meriwether was happy to be in the saddle again. He hoped to have everything organized so that he could be headed for Pittsburgh to start the expedition by the end of April, when the trail over the Appalachians would again be passable. If all went according to plan, by August 1 the Corps of Discovery might just make it to the head of the Missouri River, where they could find a good site to winter over.

The man he had chosen to build the metal-framed canoe did not, however, share Meriwether's sense of urgency. Much to Meriwether's dismay, the man had barely begun work on the boat. Meriwether soon found out why. The boat maker had never built an iron frame before, and he did not have the skills to properly read the plan and understand the technical drawings. By the time Meriwether found this out, it was too late to fire the man and find another craftsman. Meriwether decided the only thing he could do was stay in Harpers Ferry and supervise the boat builder every day until he finished the frame.

The job progressed slowly, and Meriwether was distressed as he watched first one week, then two, then three go by. He knew that President Jefferson expected him to be in Philadelphia by now, but he also knew that if he left, he could not guarantee that the frame would be finished on time.

While he waited in Harpers Ferry, Meriwether began choosing weapons for the trip. He had a letter from Secretary of War Henry Dearborn giving him permission to order anything he needed from the army arsenal located there. He chose a swivel gun that would be mounted on the keelboat and used in case of a mass attack by Indians. As a backup for the swivel gun, he selected unwieldy blunderbusses, in addition to 15 each of powder horns, bullet pouches, and gun slings, 30 brushes and wires for cleaning rifles, 500 English flint rifles, and 125 muskets. He also ordered 420 pounds of sheet lead to be melted down into shot balls, a pair of horse rifles, and 176 pounds of the best imported gunpowder.

The gunpowder was to be stored in fifty-two watertight lead canisters. With meticulous attention to detail, Meriwether calculated that when each empty canister was melted down, it would provide the right weight of metal to be molded into an even number of rifle balls. Of course he field-tested every single item before ordering it. He was determined to have the best and most modern equipment possible. And just in case they ran out of gunpowder along the way, Meriwether used his own money to buy the very latest weapon—an air rifle that did not need gunpowder to propel the bullet from its barrel.

Meriwether tried to think of every possibility and to carefully weigh the value of every single item he ordered. After all, on occasion his men would have to carry or drag every piece of equipment across unknown terrain.

Finally, on April 12, 1803, with little work left to do on the iron-frame canoe, Meriwether felt free to move on to Lancaster, Pennsylvania. On the way there he stopped in Frederickstown, Maryland, where he ordered two hundred pounds of "portable soup"—a mixture of dried beans and dried vegetables that could be boiled with water to make a nutritious meal. Meriwether had often carried portable soup with him when he was army paymaster, and he considered it one of the most important items he had ordered so far for the trip.

When he arrived in Lancaster, Meriwether went straight to the home of Andrew Ellicott, America's leading astronomer and a personal friend of Thomas Jefferson. Dr. Ellicott had already received a letter from the president asking him to help Meriwether learn all he needed to know about navigating from the stars and the sun.

The two men spent many hours practicing calculations using a sextant, a chronometer, a surveyor's compass with a ball and socket, a two-pole chain, and a set of plotting instruments. The crash course in navigation took three weeks, at the end of which Dr. Ellicott was pleased with the progress of his pupil.

With navigational skills in hand, it was time for Meriwether to journey on to Philadelphia, where Jefferson had set up the next appointment for him. This time Meriwether met with William Patterson, an expert in selecting navigation equipment. Together they went to South Third Street, where Patterson pointed out the most accurate chronometer money could buy. At $250 it was not cheap, but Meriwether knew how important a clock would be in establishing longitude and making accurate maps, and so he gladly paid the asking price. It was by far the most money he paid for a single item that he planned to take with him.

Meriwether then moved on to meet with Dr. Benjamin Rush, who along with the president had been a signer of the Declaration of Independence. Dr. Rush was the United States' most respected physician, and Meriwether was eager to ask his advice on what medicines he should take along on the journey. Dr. Rush had concocted pills that he claimed could cure just about any ailment. He called them "Rush pills," and they consisted of six parts mercury and one part chlorine. And "Rush" was the right name for them because they were potent purging pills. They set off something of an explosion in the stomach, causing its contents to be emptied in a matter of seconds.

Meriwether ordered six hundred Rush pills along with thirty other kinds of drugs. He also ordered lancets, syringes, bandages, tourniquets, and forceps. Like many other frontiersmen, Meriwether was capable of setting a bone or digging a bullet out of a man's chest. These skills, along with the herbal medicines he had learned about from his mother, made Meriwether feel confident he could handle most of the medical situations they would encounter.

Like everyone else who knew of the expedition, Dr. Rush had his own set of questions he wanted Meriwether to answer along the way. He had arranged his questions into lists concerning the moral, religious, and medical practices of the Indians. He wanted to know such detailed information as what an Indian's pulse might be in the morning and in the evening, and whether it rose immediately after eating. He also wanted to know if they practiced suicide or murdered each other, as well as how often they bathed.

Meriwether tucked the list into his coat pocket and agreed to do all he could to answer the questions. He also promised to look out for signs of the Jewish religion on the western plains. Like many other well-read men of the time, Dr. Rush believed that the fabled "Lost Tribe of Israel" might well be wandering around out there somewhere.

By now Meriwether's mind was bursting with all the new skills and information he had acquired. But Jefferson had arranged more tutorials for him. Meriwether's next stop was at the home of Dr. Benjamin Barton, a professor of botany at the University of Pennsylvania. Dr. Barton lived just a few houses down from Independence Hall. He showed Meriwether how to preserve plant and animal specimens and how to label and keep them safe while traveling over rough terrain. He also gave Meriwether lists of scientific words and their definitions, which he could use to write precise descriptions of all he saw.

Meriwether's last stop in Philadelphia was a visit with Dr. Casper Wistar, an expert in fossils. Dr. Wistar talked to Meriwether about how to excavate fossils and pack them. He had high hopes that the expedition would uncover some major fossil sites and maybe even find a few live mastodons left over from the prehistoric age. Meriwether was not so excited about this thought. He wondered how effective his weapons would be against such a massive creature!

By June 7 Meriwether had achieved all he had set out to do in Philadelphia. It was time to travel back to Washington to make the final arrangements. He arranged for the thirty-five thousand pounds of goods he had ordered so far to be taken by wagon to Pittsburgh, where he hoped to pick them up within a week or so.

As he journeyed back to Washington, Meriwether thought about the men he wanted to accompany him on the expedition. There was one man who Meriwether knew would be perfect for the job. That man was Captain William Clark, whom Meriwether had served with in the Chosen Rifle Company. William Clark was a brave and unflappable leader who won the respect and allegiance of all who served under him. What's more, Meriwether enjoyed his company, and since the group of men would be together twenty-four hours a day for the next eighteen months, that was an important consideration.

Before he arrived back in Washington, Meriwether made an unusual decision for a military man. One of the first lessons a recruit learns in the military is the chain of command. Everyone knows exactly whom he must report to and obey. There is only one leader, and he bears responsibility for everything that goes on under his command. However, Meriwether decided to dispense with this tradition. He would ask Jefferson for permission to offer William Clark the position of co-leader of the expedition. Lewis and Clark would both have the rank of captain and would both make decisions about how they should proceed. If they could not agree, they would talk it out until they did because neither man would be able to pull rank on the other.

Meriwether wanted the leadership for the expedition to be this way for several reasons. He trusted William Clark's judgment as much as his own. He also was realistic enough to know that he could be killed on the expedition, in which case it would be easier on the men knowing they had another leader with them. And there might be times along the way when the expedition needed to split into two groups, in which case Meriwether could lead one group and William Clark the other.

The next time Meriwether saw the president, he asked if William Clark could be made his co-captain. Jefferson raised his eyebrows slightly and then told Meriwether he had permission to do whatever he thought was best for the expedition. So on June 19, 1803, Meriwether Lewis wrote to his old friend William offering him the position. He instructed William, if interested, to send his reply to the army fort in Pittsburgh, since Meriwether hoped to arrive there soon.

Once back in Washington, Meriwether seemed to have a million last-minute details to attend to. He wrote to his mother to apologize for not being able to get back to Locust Hill to visit as he had promised. He just had too much to do.

Finally Monday, July 4, 1803, rolled around. The day marked the celebration of the twenty-seventh anniversary of the founding of the United States, and it proved to be a dramatic day. It was the day Meriwether Lewis finally set out from Washington on the first leg of his journey across the North American continent to the Pacific Ocean. It was also the day the United States government announced it had purchased all of Louisiana Territory from the French. No one could have imagined such a thing. Countries gained land by invading other countries and declaring war, not by anything as dignified as handing over a check and giving a handshake. But it was true. Louisiana was now part of the United States.

The success of the Monroe Project came about because at the time that James Monroe had set out for France to buy New Orleans, Napoleon had decided to resume his war on England. What Napoleon needed was money to keep his army and navy fighting, not a huge tract of land that he had no way of protecting or developing. So, much to Monroe's surprise, France offered to sell all of Louisiana to the United States for fifteen million dollars. Congress agreed to the sum, and the deal was done.

Meriwether Lewis and the Corps of Discovery now had a much greater responsibility than before. From the Mississippi River west all the way to the Continental Divide, they would be exploring land that now belonged to the United States. Every person they met along the way—trappers, traders, and Indians—were now on American soil. As a result Jefferson gave Meriwether some last-minute instructions. The Indians were to be told that their "great white father" was now the president of the United States, not the king of England or the emperor of France. Most important, Meriwether was to map the new western boundary of the United States, as no European had ever traveled overland that far west.

In one land deal, the United States had more than doubled its size, and everyone was counting on Meriwether Lewis to tell them exactly what they had purchased with their money.

Chapter 7

Frustration and Despair

A sense of relief flooded through Meriwether Lewis as the streets of Washington gave way to the open trails that led westward. At last all of the planning was behind him, and he was on his way! He set his horse to an easy canter and headed toward the Appalachian Mountains. Every so often he glanced behind him at the saddlebags hanging over the horse's rump. In the right saddlebag were three documents crucial to the success of the expedition.

The first document was an open letter to any army commander whom Meriwether met on the way to St. Louis. Secretary of War Henry Dearborn had signed the document, which informed the commander that Meriwether would be selecting men from among the soldiers under his command who would be suitable to accompany Meriwether on a journey westward. The letter read: "If any in your Company should be disposed to join Capt. Lewis, you will detach them accordingly."

Part of the letter was specifically addressed to Captain Bissell at the Kaskaskia post on the Mississippi River, downstream from St. Louis. It instructed him to provide Meriwether with eight strong men who knew how to row a boat to help ferry provisions to the expedition's winter quarters on the Missouri River and then return to their post.

Furthermore, Meriwether was authorized to offer any enlisted man who joined the Corps of Discovery six months' pay in advance, with the balance of his pay and clothing allowance handed over when he returned. The men would also receive an immediate discharge from the military upon their return, along with a generous land grant. Meriwether was also allowed to recruit nonmilitary men if he wanted and was authorized to offer them six months' pay in advance, with the balance and a bonus paid upon their return.

The second document Meriwether carried with him was much longer and was written by Thomas Jefferson. This letter, addressed to Meriwether Lewis, Esquire, Captain of the First Regiment of Infantry of the United States of America, spelled out exactly what Meriwether's mission was and how he was to conduct the men on the expedition. It listed many important issues that Meriwether and the president had talked about, including the necessity of making accurate maps; collecting samples of the various soil types, plants, and animals encountered along the way; and taking note of the climate changes the expedition passed through. It also had specific instructions on how to behave toward the Indians they met along the way. These instructions read:

> In all your intercourse with the natives, treat them in the most friendly and conciliatory manner which their own conduct will admit; allay all jealousies as to the object of your journey; satisfy them of its innocence; make them acquainted with the position, extent, character, peaceable and commercial dispositions of the United States; of our wish to be neighborly, friendly and useful to them.... If a few of their influential chiefs, within practicable distance, wish to visit us, arrange such a visit with them, and furnish them with authority to call on our officers on their entering the United States, to have them conveyed to this place at the public expense. If any of them should wish to have some of their people brought up with us, and taught such arts as may be useful to them, we will receive, instruct, and take care of them.

Jefferson went on in his letter to urge Meriwether not to take too many risks. He pointed out:

> In the loss of yourselves we should lose also the information you will have acquired.

By returning safely with that, you may enable us to renew the essay [attempt] with better calculated means. To your own discretion, therefore, must be left the degree of danger you may risk, and the point at which you should decline; only saying, we wish you to err on the side of your safety, and to bring back your party safe, even if it be with less information.

The third document was one Meriwether knew he had to protect at all cost. Men would kill to get their hands on such a document. Dated July 4, 1803, it was an open letter from Thomas Jefferson, instructing the reader to provide anything Meriwether Lewis asked for, with a promise that the United States government would repay any debt he entered into. The letter ended by saying,

I also ask of the Consuls, agents, merchants & citizens of any nation to furnish you with those supplies which your necessities may call for.... I Thomas Jefferson, President of the United States of America, have written this letter of general credit for you with my own hand, and signed it with my name. Th. Jefferson.

These three documents reminded Meriwether of the incredible trust that had been placed in him. He was able to employ any man he wanted, he could make his own decisions about whether or when to turn back, and he had what amounted to a blank check from the president himself. Now all he needed was to get to Pittsburgh, pick up the large keelboat he had ordered to be built, find some adventurous men, and head on down the Ohio River. If William Clark agreed to come along, Meriwether would pick him up at Clarksville, on the northern bank of the Ohio across from Louisville, Kentucky.

If all went well—and Meriwether was sure it would—the Corps of Discovery would travel as far as the confluence of the Mississippi and Missouri Rivers by September. This schedule would still give them two months to start up the Missouri River before cold weather forced them to stop and winter over.

The weather got hotter as Meriwether rode inland, but far from wearing him down, the journey made him more eager to get on the river and on his way. Meriwether arrived in Pittsburgh at two o'clock in the afternoon on July 15 and immediately wrote a letter to President Jefferson. Although the trail had been hot and dry, he told the president, "Yet I feel myself much benifitted by the exercise the journey has given me, and can with pleasure announce, so far all is well."

Had Meriwether waited a day, he might have written quite a different letter! It was vital that he and any men he had recruited start down the Ohio River within the next two or three days because the water level was dropping quickly and soon it would be too low for a boat to navigate. Meriwether did not want to spend the winter in Pittsburgh with such an adventure awaiting him. But as Meriwether strolled down to the riverfront early the next morning, he was in for a shock. As he neared the boat builder's yard located just downstream from where the Allegheny and Monongahela Rivers flowed together to form the Ohio River, he expected to see a large keelboat at anchor. However, he saw no such boat. Puzzled, he walked into the boat builder's yard. In front of a ramshackle wooden building, he found two men sitting on barrels playing cards.

"So what do you want?" asked the older of the two men, barely looking up from his cards.

"I'm Captain Lewis, and I believe you have a keelboat ready for me." Meriwether watched as the man motioned for the younger man to go inside.

"Ah, well, it's not been an easy task..." said the older man, standing up. "My name is Howard Jennings, at your service."

Meriwether took a step back. The smell of rum on the man's breath was overpowering. "What do you mean, it's not been an easy task?" he asked, aware that his voice was shaking.

"Well, it's on account of the lumber. Good straight lumber is in short supply right now, and though I've searched high and low for it, it's only been a week since I got enough to start on your boat.... But I have put building it at the top of my list, of course, seeing how it is for the army."

Meriwether wanted to grab Jennings by the collar and lift him off the ground. Instead he took several deep breaths. "So you won't have the boat ready by July 20 as the contract states?" he asked.

"Not likely," Jennings replied. "Of course, I am working as hard as I can on it. As I said, it's my top priority."

Meriwether looked down at the cards and the half-empty rum bottle that poked out from behind a pile of wood. What could he do? Jennings had already been paid half the money to build the boat, and it was unlikely Meriwether could find anyone else to do the job at such short notice. He would simply have to wait while it was built and make the best of his time in Pittsburgh.

"I can have the boat built by the end of the month," Jennings said, wiping sweat and grime from his brow with the back of his sleeve.

"You will if I have anything to do with it," Meriwether replied stiffly. "I order you to hire more men to work on the boat. There will be no more card games until it's finished."

"I understand," Jennings replied sheepishly. "I'll send my man out with a notice I want to hire more men, and then I'll get back to work."

"You'd better. I will be back at noon, and I expect to see a team of workers," Meriwether said, glaring at the boat builder before he turned and walked away.

As he strode back to his rooming house, Meriwether rubbed his temples with his hands. It was obviously going to be a struggle to get the keel-boat completed.

While he waited in Pittsburgh, Meriwether recruited seven soldiers from the fort there to sail the keelboat downriver with him and then return to their post—if only the boat was ready! Meriwether spent hours each day alternately threatening and pleading with Jennings to work faster. By July 29 he began to despair that the job would ever be finished. He was beside himself with worry when a letter arrived from William Clark.

Meriwether's heart beat wildly as he held the letter in his hand. Somehow he felt that if William came along with him on the expedition, in time everything would work out. But had his old friend decided to come along? Meriwether broke the wax seal, unfolded the letter, and began to read. "I will cheerfully join you my friend," wrote William. "I do assure you that no man lives with whom I would prefer to undertake such a trip as yourself. My friend, I join you with hand and heart."

Meriwether's spirits soared. Finally he had some good news. He immediately picked up a pen and wrote back. "I could neither hope, wish, nor expect from a union with any man on earth more perfect support or further aid in the discharge of the several duties of my mission than that which, I am confident, I shall derive from being associated with yourself."

In his letter, Meriwether went on to ask William to look for suitable men to join the expedition and to put off any "soft-palmed gentlemen" who, lured by unrealistic dreams of adventure and fame, might be tempted to volunteer.

Meriwether sealed the letter with wax and sent it off to William. Then it was time to divert his attention back to getting the keelboat built. Days dragged into weeks, and Meriwether continued to bully Howard Jennings and his workers to finish the boat. To keep himself company during this time, Meriwether bought a large black Newfoundland dog. He named the animal Scannon, and from that time on the two of them were inseparable.

At seven in the morning on August 31, 1803, six weeks after Meriwether had arrived in Pittsburgh, the keelboat was finally moored beside the dock ready for service. It was an impressive sight, with a shallow draft of three feet when loaded. It was fifty-five feet long and eight feet wide and had a thirty-two-foot mast that could support a square sail. The mast was designed so that it could be laid down flat if need be. At the back was an elevated deck covering a cabin. Between the cabin and the ten-foot-long deck at the bow was a thirty-one-foot-long hold that could accommodate cargo weighing up to twelve tons. Although the boat had a mast and sail, it could also be rowed, poled, and pulled, and the men would use all four means of conveyance on the trip to the headwaters of the Missouri River.

To keep the boat as light as possible at the start, Meriwether ordered that many of the heavier items for the trip be hauled downriver by wagon to Wheeling, Virginia, where the water of the Ohio River was a little deeper and faster flowing. Also to help lighten the load, Meriwether hired a pirogue, a square flat-bottomed boat, to accompany them and carry some of their provisions.

Within minutes of the keelboat's completion, cargo was being loaded aboard the boat, and by eleven o'clock that morning, everything was stowed and they were ready to cast off for the trip downriver.

In addition to the seven soldiers, on board were a pilot and the first two volunteers for the Corps of Discovery—John Colter and George Shannon. Colter was a twenty-eight-year-old private who was reputed to be one of the best hunters in the area. Shannon was only eighteen, but he had impressed Meriwether with his quiet determination and tales of growing up on the frontier in Ohio. He reminded Meriwether a lot of himself at that age. Meriwether was sure he had recruited two good men for the corps, and he hoped William Clark had found several more.

"I'd have to say I don't like our chances," the pilot said, shaking his head as Meriwether climbed aboard the boat. "I've been on this river for twenty years, and I've never seen it this low."

"We're going anyway!" Meriwether snapped. "I don't care if we only make a mile a day, we are on our way west."

Meriwether gave the order for the boat to cast off, and they began their journey down the Ohio River.

The keelboat, with the pirogue in tow, made steady progress with the soldiers rowing and the pilot guiding the rudder. Meriwether stationed himself at the bow, where he kept a lookout for submerged logs and shallow water. They had gone about three miles when he noticed the keelboat was listing. "Put in at the next dock we come to," he ordered. "We'll have to rearrange the cargo. It's not balanced right."

Around the next bend in the river was a dock, and soon the boat was tied up and the crew was busy moving some of the heavier bales of provisions from the port to the starboard side. Several men came out from a nearby cabin to help. When the cargo had been rearranged to Meriwether's satisfaction, Meriwether thanked the helpers.

"So what do you have there?" asked one of the helpers, staring at the air rifle that was propped up outside the cabin door.

"It's a most amazing invention," Meriwether replied. "It uses compressed air instead of gunpowder to shoot the bullet."

"Air?" questioned the man.

"Certainly does. Here, I'll show you," Meriwether said. "It doesn't even make a loud noise."

With that Meriwether picked up the rifle and strolled over to a tree. He took aim and fired seven shots at a range of fifty-five yards. He hit the post he was aiming for each time.

"Well, who would have believed it!" the man exclaimed. "How heavy is it?"

Meriwether handed the rifle to the man, who turned it over in his hands.

Hiss! Pop!

The air rifle accidentally discharged. Meriwether watched in horror as he saw a woman about forty yards away fall to the ground. Blood gushed from under the brim of her bonnet. A toddler in her arms screamed.

For a brief moment Meriwether was too stunned to move. Was this innocent bystander the first casualty of the expedition?

Chapter 8

Downriver

Y ou've killed her!" yelled an old man.
Meriwether rushed over to the unconscious woman and knelt beside her. He pressed his kerchief against the side of her head to stem the bleeding. When the blood flow had subsided, he cautiously studied the wound. Relief flooded through him. "She's going to be all right!" Meriwether announced as the woman began to stir. "The bullet only grazed her head. It's a surface wound."

Meriwether stayed just long enough to dress the woman's wound. As soon as he was done, he ordered his men back on the boat. He hardly dared think of what might have happened if the air gun had killed the woman. He promised himself he would run proper training drills with the air rifle before any of his men touched or used it.

The Ohio River was well mapped, and the pilot intimately knew its every rapid, shoal, and bend. The first major obstacle they had to navigate was the riffle off McKee's Rock. A riffle was a shallow area in the river where the rocks and stones of the riverbed caused the water to ripple as it flowed over them.

"Just as I warned you," the pilot told Meriwether as they approached McKee's Rock. "The riffle is too wide to navigate around. There's only one way to get by. You'll have to order all hands overboard."

Meriwether peered down at the water. He could see the gravelly bottom of the shoal. The pilot was right. "Into the water, men. We'll have to lift the boat up and over," he ordered.

The men obediently jumped over the side of the keelboat into waist-deep water. Meriwether followed them. They lined up on both sides of the boat, reached down, and gripped the hull.

"On my mark," Meriwether yelled. "One, two, three…heave!"

The men groaned as their arms strained. The boat began to rise and lunge forward until the men could hold it no longer. They let go, and the boat's hull settled on the stony riverbed.

"Again," ordered Meriwether after the men had repositioned themselves and gotten another grip. "One, two, three…heave!"

Once more the men groaned as they lifted the boat off the bottom and heaved it forward. It took over an hour to get the boat over the thirty-yard-long riffle. Exhausted, the men scrambled back onto the boat and took up their positions at the oars.

A mile downstream they encountered a second riffle and then a third. Each time the procedure was the same. All hands climbed overboard and carried the boat over the shallows. As they did so, Meriwether grew more and more exasperated. If the two boat builders had finished their work on time, he would be in St. Louis by now.

At seven o'clock that night, after traveling a total of ten miles, they tied the boat up at the river's edge and made camp. The men barely had the energy to drive the tent pegs into the ground. By eight o'clock Meriwether had doled out the day's whiskey ration, and everyone but the night watchman was asleep.

The following morning Meriwether awoke to the sound of water falling on his tent. Rain! Wonderful rain that would raise the level of the river. He opened the tent flaps to take a look. Much to his surprise, all he could see was a blanket of white fog. It wasn't raining at all. The fog was so thick that it had formed into water droplets on the overhanging trees, and what sounded like rain were the drops dripping off the trees and onto his tent.

Meriwether had never seen fog so thick before. He realized it would be impossible to get on their way downriver until the sun rose high enough to burn off the fog. So much for an early start!

It was eight o'clock before there was enough visibility for them to cast off again in the boat. Everyone was wearing damp clothes, a combination of not getting completely dry after jumping into and out of the river the day before and the remnants of the damp fog.

As Big Horse Tail Riffle approached, Meriwether and his men braced themselves for another day of wrestling their boat over the shallow shoals. Big Horse Tail Riffle turned out to be aptly named. It was longer than any of the riffles from the day before. This time the men had to unload the cargo onto the bank so they could lift the boat high enough in the water to get it over the shallows. The pilot estimated it would take them about two hours to drag the boat over the riffle, and he was right. Once the boat was reloaded, it was time to row on downstream to the dreaded Woolery's Trap.

The riffle at Woolery's Trap was an obstacle that proved to be too much for the boat, loaded or empty, and Meriwether had to hire a team of oxen to help pull the boat over the shallows. The oxen and the men worked together and eventually succeeded, but not before Meriwether had become very frustrated with the owners of the oxen. A group of them sat together on the riverbank and yelled contradictory advice, and they laughed uproariously as the men struggled and strained to move the boat forward. To make matters worse, they sat under huge buckeye trees whose leaves were starting to turn orange, a visible reminder that fall was quickly approaching.

In camp that night, with Scannon lying contentedly at his feet, Meriwether wrote the second entry in his journal of the trip. It read: "The inhabitants who live near these riffles live much by the distressed situation of travelers, are generally lazy, charge extravagantly when they are called

on for assistance, and have no philanthropy or
conscience."

The next day, and the day after that, they
encountered more riffles. And each time they had
to unload and reload the boat, which meant hiring
more expensive oxen teams. Meriwether became
increasingly irritated as he noticed the river level
was dropping about two inches a day.

Pushing, pulling, paddling, and poling, the men
finally coaxed the boat as far as Wheeling, Virginia,
a village of about fifty houses on the east bank of
the river. Waiting there for Meriwether was the
cargo he had sent on ahead from Pittsburgh. To
keep the weight down in the keelboat, Meriwether
hired another pirogue to help carry the goods
downstream. On September 8, after a day of rest in
Wheeling, they continued on downriver. The two
pirogues laden with cargo followed the keelboat.

There were not as many riffles in the river below
Wheeling, and the men began to make better time,
covering about twelve miles a day, that is, until one
of the pirogues sprung a leak and filled with water.
The men worked together to pull the craft ashore,
but not before everything in it was soaked.

Meriwether ordered another day of rest from
traveling while the contents of the pirogue were
laid out in the sun to dry. The damage to the cargo
was worse than he had imagined. The knives and
other iron objects he had planned to trade with the
Indians were beginning to rust, and after the items
were dry, it took the rest of the day to file off the
rust and oil them.

The next day the men proceeded on downriver. As more and more tributaries ran into the Ohio, the current grew stronger, and the men didn't have to row as hard. At one point a stiff breeze sprung up, so the men hoisted the canvas square sail. The keelboat skimmed down the river at a fast clip, but after several miles, the mast began to bend precariously, and Meriwether ordered the sail taken down before the mast snapped. The men went back to rowing.

Although there were fish in the river and an abundance of wildlife along the shore, Meriwether could not spare any of his men to fish or hunt. All hands were needed on deck to keep the boat moving. Even Scannon the dog had to earn his keep. Meriwether noticed black squirrels migrating across the river, and he would order Scannon overboard. The dog understood his mission, and a few minutes later he would scamper back on board with a dead squirrel lodged firmly in his jaw. He would drop the animal at Meriwether's feet and wag his tail before plunging back into the river for his next victim. That night the men sat around the campfire dining on roasted squirrel, which they washed down with their ration of whiskey.

On September 28, the keelboat and two pirogues reached Cincinnati. It had taken them twenty-eight days to travel five hundred miles. In Cincinnati Meriwether gave his men some much deserved leave and used his time to write letters and load up more supplies. On October 4, they set out again and headed for the Falls of the Ohio, one hundred miles downstream. The Falls of the Ohio was not really a waterfall but a two-mile-long stretch of churning rapids, during which the Ohio River dropped twenty-four feet.

Taking the boat and canoes down the rapids was a hair-raising venture made worse by the low water level. However, under the guiding hand of their pilot, the keelboat and pirogues made it safely through the rapids.

Below the rapids, on the east bank of the river, lay the town of Louisville, Kentucky. Immediately across the river on the west bank in Indiana Territory was Clarksville. Clarksville was named after Revolutionary War hero General George Rogers Clark, William Clark's older brother.

As soon as the boat and canoes were safely moored at the side of the river, Meriwether went in search of the Clark home. He soon found the place, and on the steps of the grandest house in town, he met and embraced his old friend William. The two men were now officially partners, co-captains and allies.

Meriwether and William had much to talk about as they sat out on the veranda late that afternoon. Foremost in the discussion was the selection of men for the expedition. William had put the word out that they were looking for a few adventurous young men, and hundreds had rushed to sign up. Together, over the next few days, the two men interviewed all of the volunteers, looking for those men who were strong enough to not only endure the trip but also take hardships in stride. It was difficult to choose, but after two weeks they had decided on nine men, including Charles Floyd and Nathaniel Pryor, whom they made sergeants. All nine men, along with John Colter and George Shannon, were sworn into the army in a ceremony witnessed by General Clark. The Corps of Discovery was finally a reality.

There was one more member of the corps, though he did not volunteer and was not sworn into the army. His name was York, and he was William's personal servant—a black slave who had been given to William when they were both small boys. York went everywhere with William, so it was natural that he should be included in the expedition.

On October 26, 1803, the Corps of Discovery set out from Clarksville headed for Fort Massac, located several miles upstream from where the Ohio River joined the Mississippi. The fort would mark the farthest point south the expedition would travel. At Fort Massac they intended to pick up eight soldiers who had volunteered for the expedition from the army fort at South West Post in eastern Tennessee.

South of Clarksville, travel on the river was much easier. And once they were under way, Meriwether and William began to mold the men into a tight-knit company. By the time they reached Fort Massac sixteen days later, they were beginning to function as a real team.

Unfortunately the volunteers from South West Post were not waiting for them at the fort. Meriwether hired George Drouillard, a half-French, half-Shawnee Indian hunter and scout to go to

Tennessee and find them. Since the Corps of Discovery could not wait for the volunteers to arrive, they decided to press on to St. Louis, located at the confluence of the Mississippi and Missouri Rivers, and set up winter camp just west of there.

Drouillard was fluent in two Indian languages as well as English and French. He also knew Plains Indian sign language. Meriwether and William were so impressed by his eagerness to help that they hired him as an interpreter and hunter for the expedition.

Although Fort Massac was located on a bank high above the river, it was surrounded by low-lying swampland that produced swarms of mosquitoes. Indeed, mosquitoes had been a constant pest ever since Meriwether left Pittsburgh, but now, day and night the air seemed to be constantly abuzz with them. To help ward off the mosquitoes, the men used "voyager's grease," a sticky mixture of tallow and hog's lard that they slathered on their exposed skin.

On November 13, they left Fort Massac and headed for the junction of the Ohio and Mississippi Rivers, where they made camp. Since the longitude and latitude of this spot was known, Meriwether spent some time practicing the new skills he had learned from Andrew Ellicott back in Lancaster, Pennsylvania. He tried establishing latitude and longitude to see if he could come up with the same coordinates as those that had been established for the junction of the two rivers. It wasn't easy, especially when he discovered that the accurate

chronometer he had bought in Philadelphia wasn't
so accurate and he had to take readings from the
stars to confirm his calculations. Eventually,
though, he managed to work out the correct coordinates. Using his surveying equipment, he was
also able to work out that the Mississippi was
2,002 yards wide where the Ohio River joined it.

While camped at the confluence of the two
rivers, Meriwether began to feel weak—he had contracted malaria. To help quell the disease, he began
treating himself with Dr. Rush's pills, which, in
turn, only made him feel weaker, so weak that he
couldn't stand up.

Still, Meriwether did not complain. This kind of
sickness was to be expected on such a difficult trip.
Almost everyone who ventured inland contracted
malaria, though no one knew exactly what caused
it. Meriwether suspected it had something to do
with the mistletoe that grew in the trees along the
edges of the river.

After several days, Meriwether felt strong
enough to travel again, and the Corps of Discovery
began the journey up the Mississippi River.

After several hours of battling the current
upstream, William Clark, who stood at the bow
watching for uprooted trees floating downstream,
said to Meriwether, "It's not going to work. The current is too strong."

Meriwether nodded. "We are going less than a
mile in an hour," he said. "The men are worn out
already from rowing. We're going to have to zigzag
across the river at every turn so that we're in the

shelter of the bank. It's the only place where the current is slower and we have a chance of making headway."

"True enough," William said. "They're tough men, but no one can keep up this kind of effort for too long. We'll be going against the current all the way to the Continental Divide. I suspect we're going to have to double the size of the corps. We simply need more manpower."

Once again Meriwether nodded, and he then sat silently for a moment. He knew William was right, but it was a disheartening reality. More men meant more food, more guns, more clothes, and more tents.

Even rowing in the shelter of the riverbank proved difficult, and every member of Corps of Discovery was relieved when on November 28 they finally reached Fort Kaskaskia. The fort was located on the east bank of the river sixty miles south of St. Louis. While the men rested, Meriwether showed Captain Bissell, the post commander, the letter from Secretary of War Henry Dearborn giving him permission to recruit a number of soldiers from the fort to join the Corps of Discovery. Meriwether called for volunteers, and he and William then selected fourteen of them to join the corps. Most of the men they selected had strong arms!

Meriwether did not intend to take all of the men with him to the Pacific Coast. Some would be sent back when the keelboat could go no farther. They would return to St. Louis, while the rest would continue on in canoes.

It was a refreshed group of men who set out from Fort Kaskaskia, this time headed for the mouth of the Wood River, just north of St. Louis. Captain Bissell had suggested this location as a good place to spend the winter. The location had many advantages, including a nearby forest, giving them a supply of firewood, and a neighboring pioneer settlement that the men could visit.

During this leg of the trip, William took charge of the boats while Meriwether headed on horseback for St. Louis to purchase more supplies for the expedition. After being on a boat for so long, Meriwether was relieved to be riding a horse. He made good time to St. Louis, a small town of about one thousand inhabitants that stood proudly on a bluff overlooking the river.

Meriwether spent most of the winter in St. Louis, staying at the home of a rich trader, while William commanded the winter camp. The two men had agreed to this arrangement because President Jefferson had asked Meriwether to find out as much as possible about the settlers in the surrounding area. Once Louisiana officially belonged to the United States, Jefferson planned to offer the pioneers there a land exchange. He wanted the pioneers to resettle in Illinois, thus allowing all of the land west of the Mississippi River to become a huge Indian reserve. The president hoped that the Indians would slowly adjust to white ways and take up farming. And as they did so, white people would gradually move into the areas to peacefully live and work alongside the Indians.

To find out who the pioneers were, Meriwether wrote and circulated a questionnaire. As well, he kept busy negotiating the purchase of supplies: kegs of salt, flour, lard, corn, pork, and biscuits, boxes of candles, and a cannon that William wanted to mount on the keelboat.

Through the winter Meriwether gathered information and learned as much as he could from local trappers and hunters about what lay to the west. He also visited Camp Wood, the winter home of the Corps of Discovery, whenever he had time.

On March 9, 1804, an official ceremony was held in St. Louis to mark the official transfer of Louisiana to the United States. Soon after the ceremony, Meriwether returned to the Corps of Discovery. By now the snow was melting and the men were eager to be on their way. In fact they were more than eager. They were so tired of being cooped up in camp that they had become ornery. Tempers ran hot. A private threatened to kill a sergeant, and the volunteers who eventually arrived from Tennessee liked to settle their disagreements with fistfights. The only way to cure the problem was to get moving again!

By now William knew the men very well, having spent the winter with them. As a result he took the responsibility for dividing the men into groups— those who would go all the way to the Pacific Coast of North America and those who would return to St. Louis with the keelboat after they reached their next winter camp. Those men going all the way to the Pacific Coast were divided into three squads, and William chose a man to lead each squad. The squad leaders were Sergeants Charles Floyd, Nathaniel Pryor, and John Ordway. On the way up the Missouri River, those men who were going all the way to the coast would man the keelboat while the others would paddle the pirogues.

There were the inevitable delays before they got under way. Meriwether had come to expect them by now. But on May 14, William and the men loaded up the keelboat and pirogues and headed up the Missouri River a few miles to St. Charles. There they rearranged the cargo, attended church, and waited for Meriwether to join them. Meriwether had gone to St. Louis to take care of some last-minute business.

Finally on May 21, 1804, Meriwether Lewis rode into St. Charles, eager to be reunited with his men and be on his way. A crowd of about four hundred well-wishers stood on the riverbank as the men dipped their oars into the Missouri River and headed upstream. The Corps of Discovery was on its way into uncharted territory.

The boats soon rounded a bend in the river, and the men lost sight of the crowd. Their last link with civilization had been cut. They were in Indian country, and all they had was their wits and skill to make it safely across a vast continent.

Chapter 9

Upriver

In the spring of 1804 the Missouri River flowed swift and deep, fed by melting snow to the west. As the water raged through ravines, willows and cottonwood trees were dragged into the torrent. Sometimes they were pulled along by the current at up to five miles an hour, forming huge battering rams that could puncture the keelboat's hull in a second. In places where the river's flow slowed or where shoals stretched out into the waterway, the uprooted trees piles up, forming nearly impenetrable barriers that the Corps of Discovery had to pick its way through.

Every mile that the boats traveled upstream was measured in human sweat. On a good day, when the wind was behind them and the sail could be hoisted, they covered up to twenty miles.

On the worst of days, it took the men twelve hours to go ten miles. These were the days when they had to get in the river and pull the boat using a long rope attached to the mast. With their backs hunched and shoulders bleeding from rope burns, the men dragged the laden keelboat forward. York, who had enormous rippling muscles, and Alexander Willard, who was over six feet tall and powerfully built, took turns at the head of the tow rope, encouraging the others on by their sheer strength and determination.

On June 1 they reached the mouth of the Osage River and made camp for the night. By now, nine days into the expedition, everything was running like clockwork. The keelboat was tied to a tree at the river's edge, while the pirogues were hauled up onto the riverbank. Each squad had its own cook and set up its own campfire. Two of the men, the best hunters, George Drouillard and German native John Potts, had spent the day on horseback hunting game and arrived at camp with three deer they had killed. The animals were butchered and the meat handed out for the men to cook and eat. This pleased Meriwether because it meant he did not yet have to dip into the food supplies they carried with them. He was alarmed, though, at the amount the men ate. Pulling the keelboat made the men ravenous, and they consumed nine or ten pounds of meat each in the course of a day. The meat was cooked over the fire in the evening, and some of it was set aside for the men to snack on the following day, thus ensuring that precious daylight hours weren't wasted having to stop and cook lunch.

Meriwether and William were well aware of the constant potential of danger and tried to impress it upon the men. The keelboat was a virtual floating general store and armory, and any Indians who captured it would gain enough powerful weapons and trading goods to give them a tactical advantage over other tribes and any other groups of explorers who might follow the expedition west. At any moment of any day, the Corps of Discovery could be attacked. So that night, like every other night, guards were posted around the perimeter of the camp. Through the night they called to and answered each other, alert to any crackle of a twig or scurry of a raccoon.

On the morning of June 2 Meriwether ordered the men to cut down the trees around the camp. He needed a clear view of the sun to calculate the latitude and longitude of the Osage River mouth. It took two days to fell enough trees to make this possible. Although it was extra work for the men, Meriwether was a man under orders. Jefferson expected him to produce an accurate map of the area they journeyed through, and to make the map accurate, Meriwether needed to establish the latitude and longitude of important landmarks.

Once Meriwether had taken his readings, he recorded the coordinates, and the Corps of Discovery got under way upriver again. By this time William Clark had proved himself the better boatman, and so he took charge of the boats. This allowed Meriwether to spend most of his days walking the riverbank, searching for insects and animals, drawing sketches of land formations, collecting plant specimens, and looking for springs of fresh water. It was always a happy moment when he found one. The men would come ashore and drink and fill up their canteens. By June many of the men were covered with oozing boils, which Meriwether thought were probably a result of drinking the murky water of the Missouri River, laden as it was with mud and debris.

On June 12 Pierre Cruzatte, a Creole who had earned the position of head boatman, yelled, "Canoe ahead!"

Meriwether, who was onshore at the time, ran to the water's edge and peered upstream. Sure enough, two canoes were rounding a bend about four hundred yards upstream. Meriwether's heart beat fast as he tried to make out who was in the canoes. To his relief they were white trappers. Meriwether hailed them, and the canoes paddled to shore. A tall, gray-haired man stepped out of the lead canoe and introduced himself. "I am Pierre Dorion," he said in French.

"Welcome. I am Captain Meriwether Lewis, and this is my co-captain, William Clark," Meriwether replied in English.

The Frenchman raised his eyebrows in surprise and began speaking in English. "English or American?" he asked.

"American," Meriwether replied.

"And what brings a boat this size up the Missouri?" Dorion inquired.

For the next two hours the men exchanged information. Meriwether learned that Dorion was taking furs down to St. Louis. He was traveling with five other trappers and his Yankton Indian wife.

"Yankton—aren't they a tribe of Sioux Indians?" Meriwether asked.

"That's right," Dorion replied. "I've been up there since 1785. I won't say it's an easy life, but the pelts we have on board this canoe should net us about nine hundred dollars. That and the buffalo grease we're going to sell will keep us in gunpowder and provisions for a long time. Here, take a look at the quality of these pelts. You won't find any better." With that Dorion strolled over to the second canoe, slit the side of a bale with his knife, and pulled out a beaver pelt.

Meriwether ran his hand over the soft black fur. "You're right," he replied. "I haven't seen anything better. Did you say you had buffalo grease for sale?"

"Yes," the trapper replied, "one thousand pounds of it."

"Are buffalo very abundant?" Meriwether asked. He had been told that there were so many buffalo on the plains to the west that they sometimes looked like a black cloud covering the earth. He found this hard to believe, especially since he had never seen a buffalo himself.

Dorion laughed. "They stretch as far as the eye can see on a summer's day," he replied.

Meriwether arranged to buy three hundred pounds of the buffalo grease. Some of it would be used for cooking, and the rest would top off their supply of voyager's grease, since the mosquitoes were still a constant pest.

As the men talked, Meriwether's mind swirled. Dorion was just what the expedition needed. He spoke a Sioux language, and through his marriage he had become a part of the Yankton tribe. There was no one who would be better at interpreting for him and William and convincing the chief of the Yankton tribe to make a trip east to Washington to meet President Jefferson. The only problem was Pierre Dorion was headed in the opposite direction from the Corps of Discovery.

It took a lot of persuasion, but eventually Meriwether offered Dorion enough reasons to join the Corps of Discovery on its journey upriver. Convinced he should go along on the expedition, Dorion threw his pack aboard the keelboat, and soon the corps was on its way again. Meriwether could hardly believe his good fortune. Other members of the expedition spoke Shawnee, Omaha, and Plains Indian sign language, and now he had someone who could speak with the Sioux.

On the Fourth of July, the keelboat tied up for the night at the entrance to a creek, which, in honor of the day, Meriwether named Independence Creek. The keelboat's cannon was fired, and an extra ration of whiskey was metered out to the men. Around a large campfire the men danced to Private Pierre Cruzatte's fiddle playing late into the night.

As the celebrating began to subside, Meriwether marveled at how long a year could seem. It had been exactly 365 days since he had set out from

Washington on his way to Pittsburgh. As he reflected, all in all he was pleased with the way the expedition was going. The men had experienced a number of nerve-wracking setbacks at the beginning, but now that they were alone pitting their wits against nature, everything was running smoothly. Well, almost smoothly. Three days before, Meriwether had had to convene a court-martial when two of the men stole whiskey and got themselves drunk. The punishment was one hundred lashes for Private Hugh Hall, who was supposed to be guarding the stores at the time, and fifty lashes for Private John Collins, who had discovered Private Hall getting drunk and decided to join him instead of reporting him.

All of the men took turns delivering the lashings, and the two culprits were barely able to move when it was done. Meriwether blamed the whole incident on the fact that the expedition had stopped for a few nights to rest. The men were not good with too much spare time on their hands, and Meriwether began to wonder how they would get on being cooped up together at their next winter camp.

The following morning they continued the journey westward. Thankfully, the steeply wooded banks of the river were giving way to patches of open prairie, and the men did not have to tow the boat as frequently.

As the expedition moved upriver, Meriwether kept busy recording facts about the animals he saw. Most of them were known to science, but very few details were known about how they lived in the wild. Meriwether did spot one curious animal that he described in his journal as having the "Shape & Size like that of a Beaver, his head mouth etc. is like a Dogs with Short Ears, his Tail and Hair like that of a Ground Hog, and longer...his legs are short and when he moves Just sufficent to raise his body above the Ground, He is of the Bear Species." The animal he was referring to was a badger. Meriwether also spotted a coyote, which at first he thought was a fox. And when a huge cloud appeared on the horizon, everyone was amazed to see that it was a flock of pelicans. Meriwether shot one of the birds and examined it with great interest. He took all sorts of measurements, including the size of its beak to see how much liquid it would hold, which turned out to be five gallons.

As July wore on and the summer sun became intense, Meriwether found he had to allow time for the men to rest at midday. Even so, five or six men were sick at any one time, mainly from heatstroke or dysentery. Dr. Rush's pills, now aptly named "thunderclaps," were doled out for all sorts of ailments.

Men also became sick with malaria, and they were doctored with the powdered bark of a tree from South America. The bark contained quinine, which, although it did not cure the disease, helped lessen its symptoms.

As the men grew weaker, it became more difficult for them to stay awake at night on guard duty. This worried Meriwether and William because they knew how important the security of the camp was. Although no one had yet seen an Indian, the French trappers said it was only a matter of time before they would encounter some.

Meriwether did not want such an encounter with the Indians to be at gunpoint in the dead of night. So he was very upset when Alexander Willard, one of the corps's best men, was caught sleeping on duty. This was a serious infraction, one that U.S. Army regulations stated could be punished with a death sentence. Meriwether had no intention of putting one of his men to death, but everyone in the Corps of Discovery had to understand how important it was to be vigilant at all times, especially while on guard duty. A court-martial was convened, and Willard was found guilty and sentenced to one hundred lashes each evening for four days.

On July 21, sixty-eight days after leaving Camp Wood, the expedition reached the mouth of the Platte River. Meriwether had been told it marked the boundary of Oto, Pawnee, and Loup Indian lands. But where were the Indians? Meriwether climbed a bluff overlooking the river for a good view of the surrounding countryside. It was a magnificent sight. Meriwether had never before seen such an expanse of flat land without trees. Grass a foot high swayed in the breeze as far as he could see. But not an Indian was to be seen. Surely, Meriwether told William that night, they must encounter a tribe soon.

Chapter 10

Little Thief

It was a stifling afternoon on August 2, 1804. Meriwether Lewis was sitting at his portable desk writing a description of a purple coneflower when he heard a yell from the lookout.

"Captain...Indians approaching!"

Meriwether's heart quickened as he hurried to assess the situation. Sure enough, a hundred yards or so away were about seven Indian warriors and a white trader. They waved a greeting, and the trader yelled a greeting in broken English.

Meriwether ordered that the cannon be fired as a welcome salute, and the Indians appeared to appreciate the gesture. They responded by firing their rifles in the air. Afterward the warriors shook hands with Meriwether and William. The trader introduced himself as Gaston Fairfon.

By now all the men except for those on guard duty were crowded around, waiting to see what would happen. It was all very friendly. Fairfon told Meriwether that these were Oto and Missouri Indians and that a band of about 250 of them was camped several miles away. Meriwether immediately invited them to return for a council at the corps's campsite the following morning. The Indians enthusiastically accepted the invitation. William dispensed pickled pork, flour, cornmeal, and tobacco to them before they left, promising to return with their chiefs in the morning.

That night Meriwether could not sleep. It wasn't just the usual ticks and lice crawling over him that kept him awake. No, he was recalling over and over every moment of the meeting with the Indians, trying to be absolutely sure he was not being led into a trap. Was this first meeting just a way for the Indians to take a good look at the camp and see how many men there were? Meriwether decided it was best to go ahead with the council in the morning, but he would be cautious. He would post extra guards on duty and meet in the open on the sandy riverbank, which would give them some warning of an impending ambush.

Finally Meriwether drifted off into a fitful sleep, but he was up before dawn the next morning to find a dense fog hanging over the river. He lit his lamp and reread the speech he had been working on for weeks. The paper was limp from the damp air, but Meriwether felt sure that the meaning of the words recorded on the paper was crisp and clear. The speech contained all of the messages President Jefferson wanted conveyed to the Indians. Meriwether scrawled a few changes and smiled in approval at what he had written. It was a good speech and probably the most important speech he would ever deliver. He intended to repeat the speech to every tribe he met along the river.

As soon as it was light, Meriwether changed from his leather pants and jacket into his full dress uniform, complete with cocked hat and boots. He had to cinch up his belt a notch or two, but other than that everything fit perfectly.

Meriwether didn't think the Indians would arrive until the fog had burned off, and in the meantime there was work to do around camp. He ordered that the sail from the keelboat be set up as an awning so that his men and the Indians could sit in the shade. He didn't want his men sitting with their backs against any of the huge cottonwood trees that grew along the river's edge because that would only make it easier for someone to creep up from behind and ambush them. He also doubled the number of guards on duty and ordered that each man be ready to defend himself if necessary.

At ten o'clock that morning, a group of about twenty Indians and Gaston Fairfon walked back into camp. They greeted Meriwether and William as if they were old friends and laughed among themselves. It was a good sign. At least Meriwether hoped so.

William called the Corps of Discovery to attention, and the men paraded together in step, rifles held across their chests, eyes forward. Meriwether was pleased to see a nod of admiration from some of the young chiefs. It had always been part of Jefferson's plan to impress the Indians with the power and discipline of the United States Army, and Meriwether was proud to think that the Corps of Discovery had made a good first impression.

When the marching was finished, Meriwether stepped forward and prepared to deliver his speech. He adjusted his hat and pulled the folded sheets of paper containing the speech from inside his uniform jacket. He hoisted himself up straight and started to read from the paper. "Welcome to the United States. Children, commissioned and sent by the Great Chief of the Seventeen Great Nations [the states] of America, we have come to inform you as we go also to inform all the nations of red men who inhabit the borders of the Missouri, that a great council was lately held between this Great Chief of the Seventeen Nations of America and your old Fathers, the French and Spaniards, and that in this great council, it was agreed that all the white men of Louisiana inhabiting the waters of the Missouri and Mississippi should obey the commands of this Great Chief. He has, accordingly adopted them as his children and they now form one common family with us. Your old traders are of this description. They are no longer the subjects of France or Spain but have become citizens of the Seventeen Great Nations of America, and are bound to obey the commands of their Great Chief, the President, who is now your only Great Father."

Meriwether stopped to allow Fairfon time to translate his words for the Indians. This took some time, and Meriwether began to wonder just how accurate the translation was. One or two words spoken wrongly and the importance of what he was saying could be lost. But what could he do? There was no way to check whether his words were being translated correctly, or even if the French trader was willing to tell the Indians they were all now subjects of the United States. As Fairfon spoke, several of the Indians eyed the bale of goods that William would distribute at the end of the speech. Meriwether wished they would concentrate on what was being said instead.

Eventually the translation was over, and Meriwether resumed speaking. "Children, the Great Chief of the Seventeen Great Nations of America, impelled by his parental regard for his newly adopted children on the Troubled Waters, has sent us to clear the road, remove every obstruction, and to make it the road of peace between himself and his red children residing there, to enquire into the nature of their wants and, on our return, to inform him of them in order that he may make the necessary arrangements for their relief."

Meriwether drew a deep breath before continuing. "He has commanded us, his war chiefs, to undertake this long journey, which we have so far accomplished with great labor and much expense, in order to council with yourselves and his other red children on the Troubled Waters, to give you his good advice, to point to you the road in which you must walk to obtain happiness. He has further commanded us to tell you that when you accept his flag and medal, you accept herewith his hand in friendship, which will never be withdrawn from your nation as long as you continue to follow the councils which he may command his chiefs to give you, and shut your ears to the councils of bad birds."

Again Meriwether stopped and waited for Fairfon to translate his words. He hoped the Indians were still listening, because the last part of his speech was most important. Jefferson wanted Meriwether to win the Indians over so that they would live peacefully with each other and trade fairly with American traders. But if the Indians would not do these things willingly, they would have to be forced to do so.

When Fairfon had finished, Meriwether continued, trying to sound firm but not threatening. "You are to live in peace with all the white men, for they are his children; neither wage war against the red men, your neighbors, for they are equally his children and he is bound to protect them. Injure not the person of any traders who may come among you, neither destroy nor take their property from them by force, more particularly those traders who visit you under the protection of your Great Father's flag. Do not obstruct the passage of any boat, pirogue, or other vessel which may be ascending or descending the Missouri River, more especially such as may be under the cover of your Great Father's flag, neither injure any red or white man on board such vessels as may possess the flag for, by that signal, you may know them to be good men and that they do not intend to injure you."

Meriwether stopped to let Fairfon translate, and then he continued. "Children, do these things which your Great Father advises and be happy. Avoid the council of bad birds, turn on your heels from them as you would from the precipice of a high rock, whose summit reached the clouds and whose base was washed by the gulf of human woes, lest by one false step you should bring upon your nation the displeasure of your Great Father, the Great Chief of the Seventeen Great Nations of America, who would consume you as the fire consumes the grass of the plains. The mouths of all the rivers through which the traders bring goods to you are in his possession and if you displease him, he could, at pleasure, shut them up and prevent his traders from coming among you and this would, of course, bring all the calamities of want upon you. But it is not the wish of your Great Father to injure you; on the contrary, he is now pursuing the measures best calculated to insure your happiness."

After Fairfon had translated this, Meriwether concluded his speech by telling the Indians that he was not a trader himself, but that if they did all that he said, it would not be long before the United States government set up trading posts all along the river.

The Indians smiled and nodded when they heard this. They needed to trade with white people to have weapons to protect themselves from other tribes and to wage war when necessary. If one tribe gathered more of the white man's weapons than its neighbor, the weaker tribe would inevitably be conquered, the men killed, and the women and children taken as slaves.

Having finished his speech, it was Meriwether's turn to listen. He sat quietly as one of the Indians made a speech that was translated into fractured English by Fairfon. The Indians told Meriwether that their head chief, Chief Little Thief, was out on a hunting expedition but they would tell him everything they had heard.

This upset Meriwether a little. He had wanted to reach the top man in each tribe, but there was nothing he could do about it now. He hoped he might have the opportunity to meet Chief Little Thief as the Corps of Discovery headed farther west.

The Indians promised to follow all of Meriwether's advice and obey the Great White Chief of the Seventeen Nations. They asked for white men to come and help them make peace with their neighbors, the Omaha Indians. This was exactly what Meriwether wanted to hear! His chest swelled with pride as he thought about how pleased Jefferson would be with the Indians' willingness to submit to the authority of the United States government. The Indians weren't so hard to get along with after all.

With a light heart, Meriwether watched as William took medals and tiny American flags from one of the bales of cargo and handed them around. Each medal had a silhouette of Thomas Jefferson on one side and two hands shaking, one Indian and one white, on the other. Because he was generally pleased with the way their first contact had gone, Meriwether gave the Indians a canister of gunpowder and a bottle of whiskey. He also demonstrated his air rifle so that they could see the kind of weapons they could look forward to obtaining when a trading post was set up in their territory. The Indians were most impressed by the demonstration.

Later that day William named the site of the meeting Council Bluffs, in honor of the first contact between the Corps of Discovery and the Indians.

The following day the expedition set off upriver again, though La Liberté, a Frenchman and one of the pirogue paddlers, had not returned to camp. Meriwether assumed he was safe and would find his way back to the corps in a day or two. What he didn't know was that some of the men in the Corps of Discovery were beginning to have doubts about the expedition and were eager to slip away from camp, as it turned out La Liberté had done.

Two days later the men stopped to examine an abandoned French trading post. While they were looking over the dilapidated remains, Private Moses Reed, one of the men going all the way to the Pacific Coast, approached Meriwether. "Captain, sir, my knife is missing, and I think I left it back at the campsite where we met the Indians," he said.

Meriwether shook his head. A soldier without his weapons was useless. "Go back and look for it. I expect you to take no longer than two days," he sighed.

Private Reed saluted and hurried off to get his knapsack. Meriwether was confident that Reed would easily catch up to the rest of the corps as they continued on upriver. The Missouri River was particularly meandering at this stage. Indeed at one point the river turned back on itself so much that traveling twelve miles upstream put them only 370 yards farther west!

Two days passed and there was no sign of Private Reed. Meriwether ordered the private's belongings be searched. Just as he suspected, Reed had taken everything he owned with him, as well as his army-issued rifle and a pouch of gunpowder. He had deserted! Meriwether then suspected that he had met up with La Liberté and the two men were on their way downriver.

As much as Meriwether wanted to keep pushing upriver as far as he could before winter, he was a captain in the United States Army, and he could not tolerate a deserter. If he did, the rest of the men might run off at the first sign of real trouble. Moses Reed would have to be caught and punished.

Meriwether and William agreed wholeheartedly on this point, and they dispatched four men, including their best trackers, George Drouillard and William Bratton, to find Private Reed and bring him back, dead or alive. The men were to hunt for La Liberté as well.

The Corps of Discovery made camp beside the river and waited. This delay gave the men time to fish. William and several of the men set up a fish trap made from willow branches and caught 387 fish. Meriwether experimented with a net woven together from brush and caught 709 fish. After the fish were weighed and Meriwether had sketched the various species, the men fried the fish and ate them with gusto.

On Meriwether Lewis's thirtieth birthday, August 18, 1804, the tracking party returned. They had Moses Reed with them, along with Gaston Fairfon and eight Indians, including Chief Little Thief. The group had not been able to find La Liberté.

Putting military order first, Meriwether immediately convened a court-martial. Reed pled guilty to desertion and begged for mercy. By now Meriwether had grown to appreciate all of the men, so he and William decided the appropriate punishment would not be too severe. Reed would have to run the gauntlet four times. Running the gauntlet involved all the men lining up in two rows. Reed would then walk between the rows four times while each man gave him nine lashes with a whip. In addition, Reed was removed from the permanent group of men going all the way to the Pacific Coast. He would return downriver to St. Louis with the keelboat the following spring.

Running the gauntlet was carried out right there on the spot, much to the surprise of the Indians.

"Why do you do that?" Chief Little Thief asked through Fairfon the interpreter.

Meriwether tried to explain that this was the way the Great White Chief kept his men in order, but it only made Chief Little Thief's eyes grow wider.

"We do not do this to our sons," he said. "If we break their spirits, they will never make good hunters or good chiefs. If a warrior does wrong, we may kill him, but we would never whip him."

Meriwether tried to explain further, but it was of no use, and Chief Little Thief begged him to pardon Private Reed.

Eventually Reed made his way slowly and painfully through the gauntlet for the last time. At the end he collapsed, and one of the men poured cold water over him to revive him. Meriwether hoped the punishment had not made too bad an impression on Chief Little Thief, and he ordered the men to prepare for another Indian council right away.

Once again the keelboat sail was set up as an awning, and trinkets and tobacco were pulled from bales of provisions.

Chief Little Thief sat quietly through the same speech Meriwether had given two weeks before, and he appeared to be happy with what he heard. He told Meriwether that he would consider going east to see President Jefferson. That night, in the light of a full moon, Pierre Cruzatte played his fiddle while the rest of the men danced.

Meriwether was happier with this second encounter with the Indians than with the first, though his happiness did not last long. A day later he was called to the side of Sergeant Charles Floyd. Everyone in the corps had been sick on the trip, so Meriwether was not too alarmed to hear that Sergeant Floyd was vomiting, at least not until he felt for his pulse. Meriwether had to press his fingers hard against Floyd's wrist to find his pulse, since it was so weak.

Sergeant Floyd was a very sick man, though it was uncertain what he was sick with. As far as Meriwether could tell, either some part of his stomach had burst, or he had a massive internal infection. He used the standard treatment, bleeding Floyd twice and plying him with "thunderclaps." But it was no use. On August 20, 1804, Sergeant Charles Floyd died. He was the first casualty of the Corps of Discovery.

The rest of the men were stunned. They dug a grave on a bluff overlooking their camp, which they named Floyd's Bluff in honor of the first American army officer to die west of the Mississippi. They marked his grave with wooden posts and held a military funeral service for him.

It was a somber moment. Meriwether looked at the faces of the men who made up the Corps of Discovery. Since so much danger still lay ahead before they reached the Pacific Coast, he supposed the men were all thinking the same thing: Whose life would be the next to be endangered?

Chapter 11

Sioux Territory

Meriwether Lewis and William Clark discussed who should be promoted to sergeant to replace Charles Floyd. They had several good candidates to choose from, but in the end the two co-captains made an unusual decision: They would let the men decide who should be their new sergeant. A vote was taken, and Private Patrick Gass, the Corps of Discovery's best carpenter, won. Meriwether then officially promoted him.

Three days after Sergeant Floyd's death, Joseph Fields returned to camp. He had been out hunting and brought good news: He had killed the expedition's first buffalo! Soon everyone's focus was turned from their dead comrade to the task of getting the carcass of the buffalo back to camp. Twelve men were sent out to cut up the beast and carry the meat back. Most of the men, except for the French trappers, had never tasted buffalo, and they were eager to try it, especially since now they were emerging onto the Great Plains and buffalo would be their main food source.

Huge chunks of the meat were cooked over an open fire that evening, and everyone agreed it tasted good, almost as good as beaver tail, which had been the corps's favorite meat up until then.

Two days later, when all the meat had been eaten, Private George Shannon and a nearsighted Private Pierre Cruzatte were sent out for the day to hunt more buffalo. Things did not go well for the two hunters, and just before darkness fell, Cruzatte made it back to camp on foot. When he discovered that Shannon was not there, he went straight to Meriwether.

"Captain," Cruzatte began, after he had found Meriwether sketching a picture of a bird he had just caught. "Private Shannon has not returned. We were searching for buffalo. I got off my horse and walked on ahead to see if there were any tracks. I waited for Shannon to rendezvous with me, but he never came. I retraced my footsteps all the way back here, but I have not seen him."

Meriwether frowned. "You don't know where he went?"

"No," Cruzatte replied.

Meriwether became worried. He did not want to lose another man. He went in search of William, and as the last vestiges of daylight ebbed away, the two co-captains walked along the edge of the river, puzzling over what to do about the situation.

"What do you think has happened to him?" William asked.

Meriwether shook his head. "I don't know, but I'm sure he hasn't deserted. He's out there somewhere, but where?"

"He could be anywhere. With Cruzatte's eyesight, Shannon could have been hurt or unconscious by the edge of the trail, and Cruzatte may not have noticed. I hate to think of Shannon out there alone."

"So do I," Meriwether replied. "He has a fine mind and a good education, but I don't think he can survive long on his own. He has the last two horses with him, but if he runs out of gunpowder, I don't know how he will get food. He's no woodsman."

An air of gloom settled over the two men as the muddy water of the Missouri River lapped at their feet. Meriwether thought about the young man who had joined the expedition back in Pittsburgh, before they set off down the Ohio River. Had Shannon run into trouble with Indians? Was he wounded? Had he fallen and broken his leg?

William broke into Meriwether's thoughts. "If he's not back by morning, we'll send out John Colter to look for him.

"Let's hope that won't be necessary," Meriwether responded.

Shannon had not returned by the following morning, and Colter, the Corps of Discovery's best hunter, was dispatched to find him. He returned empty-handed that night, and the next day Pierre Dorian was sent to see if he could locate Shannon. He, too, found no sign of the private.

Reluctantly Meriwether ordered the Corps of Discovery to start upriver again the next day. They had to keep moving, or they would not make it to Mandan territory by winter.

On August 27, 1804, Dorian informed Meriwether that they had passed into Yankton Sioux territory. He suggested they light a prairie fire as a sign to the Indians that white men wanted to meet them. Soon the knee-high grass was ablaze, and everyone waited on high alert to see if the Sioux responded to the "invitation." Several hours later a lone teenage boy swam out to the keelboat. Colter hauled him aboard, and using Dorian as interpreter, the boy told Meriwether that he belonged to a large band of Sioux who were camped a few miles away.

Meriwether was encouraged that the Yankton Sioux had sent an unarmed teenager to meet them. He hoped they might not be as dangerous as they had been described. He asked Dorian and Nathaniel Pryor to accompany the boy back to his camp and invite the chiefs from the group to a council under a nearby bluff, where the corps would make camp.

A sign of hope awaited the corps when they reached the bluff. On a sandy beach, one of the French trackers had spotted two sets of footprints, one human and one horse. Meriwether was cheered by the possibility they might belong to George

Shannon, though if they did, one of the horses was no longer with him. Meriwether immediately sent out one of the hunters to search for Shannon. The hunter took along extra rations in case he found him.

Although things with the Indians had gone well so far, Meriwether approached the council with the Yankton Sioux cautiously. Once again he had the men use the keelboat sail as an awning and ordered it set up in a wide clearing, and he appointed guards who would take up stations on all four sides of the awning. The men also dug a hole and dropped a small tree trunk into it to serve as a flagstaff, on which they hoisted an American flag. Once preparations were made, they waited. At four o'clock in the afternoon, as Meriwether supervised three privates who were making a new towrope from elk skin, he heard a shout from the far shore. He looked over and saw a band of about seventy Sioux warriors dressed in painted hide shirts and leggings. With them were Dorian and Pryor. A pirogue was sent across the river to bring the two members of the Corps of Discovery back safely.

As soon as they climbed from the pirogue, they reported to Meriwether how well their meeting had gone. The Yankton Sioux had treated them like royalty, covering them with buffalo robes and inviting them to feast on roast dog.

Meriwether was relieved, and he sent Dorian back across the river laden with a gift comprising corn, tobacco, and an iron kettle, along with instructions to ask the Indians to come for a council in the morning.

It was agreed, and the following morning at ten o'clock a pirogue was sent across the river to begin ferrying the Indians to the meeting place. The first to cross the river in the pirogue were the five chiefs of the tribe wearing huge feathered headbands. Accompanying the chiefs were four musicians, who shook deer-hoof rattles and beat drums as the chiefs greeted Meriwether and the other white men.

Soon the chiefs were sitting under the awning. Meriwether cleared his throat and began speaking. He gave the same speech that he had given to the Oto and Missouri Indians. With Dorian's language skill, Meriwether had no doubt that the chiefs would understand his message. When he had finished, the chiefs told Meriwether they needed a day to think about belonging to a new Great White Father. Meriwether agreed, and the council concluded with William handing out presidential medals to four of the chiefs and a red military jacket to the fifth.

It was then time for fun! The Indians appeared to be very relaxed around the men of the Corps of Discovery. The young boys fired arrows at tree limbs, showing off their expertise with bow and arrow. And when night fell, many of the older warriors painted symbols on their faces and danced around the flickering campfire. Long into the night they danced, encouraged by the trinkets and tobacco tossed at them by the soldiers.

It was a spectacular sight, one that gave Meriwether hope. Maybe things would continue to go this well. Perhaps all the Indians who lived across the plains were ready to make peace with one another and accept the authority of the president of the United States. It certainly seemed possible, judging by the response of the Indians they had contacted so far.

In the morning the chiefs gave Meriwether their answer. Yes, they were prepared to live at peace with other tribes. And yes, some of them were willing to go to Washington to meet the Great White Chief, but on the condition that the Corps leave Pierre Dorian with them for the winter. Dorian could help broker peace and escort the chiefs east to Washington. Meriwether frowned. He wondered how friendly the next band of Sioux would be, especially without his best interpreter with him. However, the chiefs would not change their minds, and Meriwether decided it was a fair request. He just hoped the Sioux farther upstream were as friendly as the Yanktons.

In early September the riverbank was teeming with animals. There was more food—deer, antelope, elk, and buffalo—than the members of the corps could eat. And where Meriwether had first seen herds of fifty or a hundred buffalo, now the animals were like black clouds on the landscape as thousands of them thundered across the prairie. It was an amazing sight.

As well as watching the buffalo, Meriwether busied himself categorizing everything he saw. He killed an antelope and a prairie dog and stuffed them, making them ready to send back to St. Louis in the spring. Neither of these animals was known to science. Meriwether even kept the animals' bones to send back as well.

On September 11 a small miracle occurred. As the keelboat rounded a bend in the river, the bowman spotted a man sitting at the river's edge. It was Private George Shannon! He was weak and near death when the men pulled him aboard the boat, but food and drink revived him. Soon he began to tell his story. Sixteen days earlier he had somehow lost his bearings and become separated from Pierre Cruzatte. Finally he found his way to the river. He was sure the Corps of Discovery had continued upstream without him, so he began following them. One horse died, and he soon used up all his shot. He managed to kill a rabbit using a long, hard stick in his rifle instead of a ball of shot. The rabbit and some wild grapes were all he'd had to eat in over a week. When the men found him, he had given up on the idea of catching up with the corps. Instead he was hoping some trappers would come by on their way downriver and take him back to St. Louis. In actual fact, Shannon had been ahead of the expedition the whole time! Meriwether and William were relieved to have him safely back.

With everyone back on board, the men of the Corps of Discovery were in good spirits. As well, a wind began to blow from the south, allowing them to hoist the sail. With the wind billowing in the sails, they were able to cover up to thirty-three miles some days.

On Sunday, September 23, the men began setting up camp as usual for the night when one of the guards yelled that three Teton Sioux boys were swimming across the river. All activity stopped as George Drouillard talked to the boys in Plains Indian sign language. The boys gestured that there was a camp of about eighty teepees at the mouth of the next river. Meriwether had Drouillard sign that the expedition would be at their village for a council the following day.

It was another restless night for Meriwether, not helped by the fact that John Colter had had his horse stolen while hunting a mile upstream. It was the last horse the expedition had brought with them from St. Charles. Meriwether hoped it wasn't an omen of trouble to come.

By late afternoon the following day the keelboat reached the Teton Sioux camp. Meriwether and William had agreed that the keelboat should stay well offshore in the middle of the river for the night.

The following morning two-thirds of the men stayed on board the keelboat to man the cannon and swivel gun if there was trouble and be ready to depart upriver at a moment's notice. The rest of the crew went ashore to act as guards for the co-captains.

A site for the council was set up onshore, with the sail once again used as an awning. An American flag was raised. The Sioux chiefs gathered under the awning, and after introductions Meriwether launched into his speech. It wasn't long, though, before he noticed that the chiefs were frowning and talking among themselves. It was soon apparent they did not understand much of what Cruzatte was saying as he interpreted the speech. Meriwether's heart sank. Cruzatte spoke only a few simple Sioux phrases, and it wasn't enough to convey the important information Meriwether wanted the Indians to have. Meriwether switched to having George Drouillard interpret using sign language, but that proved ineffective as well, and he abandoned his speech.

Meriwether began showing the Sioux chiefs various "wonders" they had brought with them—the air rifle, a magnifying glass, and a mirror. When the chiefs had finished examining these items, Meriwether gave out the usual gifts: a medal for each chief and a red uniform jacket for Black Buffalo, the man he assumed to be the leader of the tribe.

That was when the council meeting began to really go wrong. Two of the other chiefs, Partisan and Buffalo Medicine, were jealous of Black Buffalo's new coat and demanded more gifts for themselves. Meriwether decided the best solution was to separate the chiefs from the warriors and try to calm them down. He invited the chiefs back to the keelboat. The chiefs went along and were very happy when William poured them a quarter glass of whiskey each.

When the chiefs were finished, seven enlisted men were ordered to help the Indians into the pirogue and take them back to shore. But the chiefs, who were aboard a vessel carrying more trading goods than they had ever seen in their lives, did not want to go. It was a struggle to get them into the pirogue. Finally, though, the men prevailed, and William went with them as they took the chiefs ashore.

As the men paddled close to shore, where about seventy Sioux men waited, three of the warriors grabbed the bowline of the pirogue and would not let go. Then Partisan made it clear through sign language, which George Drouillard interpreted, that they would not let the men and pirogue go until they were given a canoe-load of gifts.

Meriwether watched nervously from the keelboat. "To arms!" he heard William yell from shore and watched as his co-captain drew his sword.

"Prepare for battle," Meriwether yelled to the crew. "Load the swivel gun."

The men scurried about the deck, loading musket balls into the swivel gun on the bow and tamping the blunderbusses with buckshot.

Once the guns were loaded, the men waited anxiously while Meriwether watched the Sioux warriors prepare for battle. They, too, had rifles aimed and ready and iron-tipped arrows drawn back in their bows.

Meriwether lit a taper, ready to ignite the fuse of the swivel gun. No one else moved. Both the Corps of Discovery and the Sioux warriors watched their leaders for the signal to fire.

As the tension mounted, Black Buffalo suddenly grabbed the pirogue bowline and said something to the three young warriors holding it. One by one they let go and waded ashore.

Black Buffalo turned to William and began making signs with his hands. Meriwether could not make out what he was trying to say and watched as William helped Black Buffalo into the pirogue and ordered the men to paddle to the keelboat. Meriwether was puzzled.

When they got to the boat, William informed Meriwether that Black Buffalo wanted to spend the night on board. Was it a trick? No one knew, but the two co-captains decided to allow the Sioux chief to stay on the boat. It was better if they knew where he was.

William Clark gave the order, and the men took their place at the oars. The keelboat soon began to move upriver. About a mile upstream they anchored off a sandy island, where Meriwether and William hoped they would be safe for the night. They were, and the following morning, as the keelboat slipped anchor, hundreds of inquisitive Indians lined the riverbanks. Several miles farther on, Black Buffalo, who was in a much happier mood now, signaled that he was ready to go ashore. He indicated that he was near his village and wanted William and Meriwether to go there with him.

The two co-captains held a quick conference to discuss whether they should go. If only they knew the real intentions of the Teton Sioux. Did the Indians want to steal everything the expedition owned? Or did they want to cooperate with the United States government? In the end the co-captains agreed to go along with Black Buffalo but to remain alert for trouble.

Onshore about fifty Sioux warriors came down to the riverbank, and Black Buffalo greeted them. The warriors then laid a buffalo skin on the ground and beckoned for William to sit on it. Once he did so, eight of the warriors picked up the edges of the buffalo skin and carried William over a nearby hill. As William disappeared, Meriwether quickly assigned some of the men to go and escort him to wherever the Indians were taking him.

Meanwhile Meriwether waited at the edge of the river, and an hour later the eight men came back for him. Soon he found himself sprawled on a buffalo hide being carried at shoulder height into a village of about one hundred teepees. Meriwether was gently lowered to the ground outside a brightly decorated teepee. Much to his relief, he could hear William laughing. Inside the teepee William was seated cross-legged on the floor with Black Buffalo and several of the other chiefs. A cooked dog lay between them.

"Have some dog," William said as Meriwether entered the teepee and sat down beside him.

Meriwether gave him a sympathetic look, knowing how much his partner hated to eat dog meat.

"I have some news for you," William continued. "Cruzatte has found a group of Omaha Indian prisoners, and he is trying to find a way to talk to them right now."

Meriwether nodded. This was good news indeed. Cruzatte spoke the Omaha language well, and with any luck the prisoners would be able to give the men some useful information about the Sioux.

Black Buffalo, Meriwether, and William ate and smoked peace pipes long into the afternoon, and in the evening Meriwether and William were guests at a scalp dance. Black Buffalo boasted that his warriors had raided an Omaha village just two weeks before. They had killed seventy-five Omaha men and taken forty-eight women and children prisoner. Now it was time to celebrate their great victory.

And celebrate they did. A huge bonfire was lit in a clearing, and ten musicians kept time with tambourines, rattles, and drums. The warriors began to chant, and Sioux women appeared wearing deerhide dresses heavily decorated with dyed porcupine quills. Each woman waved a long stick with one or two scalps dangling from it. These were the scalps of the Omaha men they had recently defeated. The women danced and jumped up and down in time with the drumbeat.

Meriwether found it a spectacular sight, as long as he didn't think too long about the way the Sioux seemed to revel in the destruction of their enemies. He decided to do everything he could to make sure they remained friends!

Midnight had passed before the celebration was over and Meriwether and William had the opportunity to find out what Cruzatte had learned from the prisoners. It was not good news. The Omaha Indians told Cruzatte that they had overheard Sioux braves plotting to rob the expedition and chase the Corps of Discovery back down the river.

No one slept that night, and the following day there were more talks with Black Buffalo and his men and another scalp dance in the evening. By now Meriwether was anxious to be on his way before the Indians followed through on their plan. However, he was also mindful of the need to get the Sioux to accept that they should join with Americans instead of fighting them.

On the third day, September 29, 1804, Meriwether and William decided they had done all they could to help the Sioux see this. Now it was time for them to leave, which proved difficult. The keelboat was now tied up at the shore, and as the men climbed aboard, Partisan and some of the other warriors grabbed the bowline of the boat as they had the canoe several days before. They demanded gifts before they would let go. The swivel gun was readied as tensions mounted. Finally Meriwether threw some tobacco at the men holding the line, and the men let go.

"Heave to!" William yelled, and the men began pulling hard on the oars.

The boat began to move upstream against the current. Sioux warriors stood poised on the riverbank, waiting for the signal from Black Buffalo to attack. The chief did not give it and instead let the boat move away upriver.

The Corps of Discovery had made it safely past the Sioux this time, but Meriwether worried what might happen in the spring when he planned to send the keelboat back downriver to St. Louis. What would the Teton Sioux do when they saw the boat again?

Meriwether was also frustrated because he would not be able to give a favorable report to President Jefferson that the Teton Sioux had accepted the authority of the United States. He didn't have much time, though, to dwell on how badly their encounter with the Teton Sioux had gone. It was already fall, and the expedition needed to keep moving upriver if it hoped to make it into Mandan territory before winter.

Fort Mandan

The afternoon shadows lengthened, and the nights grew colder as the Corps of Discovery paddled westward. During the first week of October they passed many abandoned Arikara villages. George Drouillard told Meriwether that smallpox was to blame. There had originally been about thirty thousand Arikara Indians, but repeated epidemics of smallpox had reduced their number to about two thousand. Some of the gardens in the deserted villages still produced corn and squash, and the men often stopped to harvest the vegetables. In many of the abandoned Arikara huts, they found human skeletons, victims of the epidemic.

On October 8 they finally met some live Arikara. An English trader named Joseph Gravelines lived

with the Arikara, and he was able to act as interpreter. This made communication with the Arikara
much easier than it had been with the Teton Sioux.
After Meriwether delivered his speech, the Indians
told him they were allied with the Sioux and at war
with the Mandan tribe upriver. Meriwether told
them that they should make peace with the
Mandan, have nothing more to do with the uncoop-
erative Sioux, and allow American boats to come up
the river. The Arikara responded positively, and
Meriwether was greatly encouraged.

After the discussion came the gift giving. Meriwether was surprised, though, at the response of
tribal leaders when they were offered whiskey.
They shook their heads. "We are astonished that
our new Great Father should offer us drink that
would make us act like fools!" they told him.

During the visit with the Arikara, York was a
great source of fascination. The Indians had never
heard of, much less seen, a black man before, and
when York realized this he decided to have some
fun. He chased the children around the camp,
making weird faces and shaking his arms in the
air. The children shrieked with fear and delight
until the noise got so loud that William ordered
him to go back to the boat.

Hawk's Feather, the Arikara chief, agreed to
Meriwether's proposal of peace with their neighbors, and one of the lesser chiefs climbed aboard
the keelboat, ready to travel upstream and meet
with the Mandan. Joseph Gravelines agreed to go
along to act as interpreter.

All of this goodwill caused Meriwether to feel optimistic. He had no idea that the Indian tribes were constantly flip-flopping between war and peace with one another. So he traveled upriver thinking he had made permanent friends with the Arikara and that they now understood it was their duty to live in peace.

On October 24 the bowman finally sighted a Mandan village on the southwest bank of the river. The Mandan village was different from anything the men had seen so far. The Sioux were nomadic, pulling up their teepees to follow the buffalo, whereas the Mandan, who also hunted buffalo, stayed in permanent villages.

The first Mandan village the men encountered was led by Chief Big White and was made up of about 130 perfectly round mud houses with domed roofs. Because the Mandan lived in permanent villages, these had become the hub of a huge trading network among many different tribes. Even British traders came down from Canada to trade with them. Because of the Mandan's reputation for being traders and friendly and accepting of foreigners, the Corps of Discovery intended to winter over in their territory.

When he saw the keelboat and pirogues, Chief Big White and twenty-five of his men made their way to the water's edge. Meriwether ordered the boats to pull ashore, and he greeted the chief. Everything went along in a friendly manner, even when the Arikara chief and Chief Big White were introduced to each other. Big White told Meriwether that he would be happy to discuss making peace with the Arikara.

While Meriwether went to the Mandan village with Chief Big White, William stayed aboard the keelboat. The two co-captains had agreed that one of them should remain with the boat at all times until it was perfectly clear that there was no threat of violence.

As they walked, Chief Big White and Meriwether talked through the interpreter Joseph Gravelines. Big White explained that the five Mandan villages in the area had a combined population of about four thousand people, thirteen hundred of whom were warriors. It did not take much calculating for Meriwether to realize that the Mandan could easily overpower the Corps of Discovery if they wanted. He determined to make it clear how dangerous it would be for the tribe to earn the anger of the Great White Father of the Seventeen Nations. However, there was no need to press this message. The Mandan were eager to trade with the "white tribe" from the east and wished them no harm.

The next day Chief Big White and the Arikara chief smoked a peace pipe together, and then the Arikara chief began the journey back to his village. With these formalities out of the way, it was time for the Corps of Discovery to find a place to set up camp for the winter. Meriwether and William chose a spot on the northeast bank of the river, opposite the village.

Fort Mandan, as they called it, was built with military precision. It had two rows of cottonwood log huts, a forge, a smokehouse, and two store-rooms all enclosed by a sturdy eighteen-foot-high log fence. The swivel gun from the bow of the keelboat was set up at the gate of the fort, and guards were on duty at all times. Although Meriwether and William were sure it was safe among the Mandan, the possibility existed that a Sioux raiding party would attack.

During the day Fort Mandan was open to visitors, and many curious Indians came to see what the white men were doing. Several traders visited, too, including a man named Toussaint Charbonneau, who immediately asked to see Meriwether.

Meriwether invited him into the hut he shared with William. Realizing the man spoke no English, he called for George Drouillard to interpret for him. The conversation began, and after a few formalities, Charbonneau explained his mission. He was a French Canadian trader who had lived with the next tribe upriver, the Hidatsa, for many years.

Unlike the Mandan Indians, the Hidatsas roamed far from home on horseback, going as far as the Rocky Mountains. Meriwether's ears pricked up at this news. He was looking for the opportunity to talk to someone who knew what lay ahead for the Corps of Discovery. But Charbonneau had some even better information. He explained that four years before, a Hidatsa raiding party had taken several Shoshone girls captive in an area known as Three Forks and returned to Hidatsa territory with them. Charbonneau had won two of the girls as a gambling prize and taken them both as his wives. Recently he had heard the Corps of Discovery would be crossing Shoshone territory, and he asked Meriwether if he wanted to hire one of his wives as an interpreter.

Meriwether tried to look businesslike, but he was delighted at this unexpected turn of events. According to the Indians, the Shoshone had a reputation for their ability to raise and trade horses, and as far as Meriwether had been able to determine, Three Forks was the name given to the place where three rivers came together to form the Missouri. Charbonneau's wives came from the place where the corps would have to abandon their canoes and continue on over the Rocky Mountains. With a Shoshone interpreter maybe they would be able to trade goods for horses so that the Corps of Discovery could proceed across the Great Divide on horseback.

Meriwether ordered one of the privates to get William Clark. When William arrived, Meriwether told him about Charbonneau's offer. It took only a minute to make a decision. The near disaster with the Teton Sioux had shown both men how important an interpreter was, even though in this case talking to a Shoshone chief would involve several steps. Charbonneau's wife would have to tell him in Hidatsa what the chief said, and then Charbonneau would have to translate the Hidatsa into French. One of the French-speaking members of the corps would then translate the French into English. Of course, the whole order would have to be reversed when Meriwether or William wanted to address the Shoshone.

"You have a deal," Meriwether said, shaking the Frenchman's hand. "Which wife will come with you?"

"Her name is Sacagawea," Charbonneau replied, "and she is due to have a baby before spring, so she will carry it with her." He waited for Drouillard to translate what he said, and then looking at the two co-captains, he added, "But don't worry about her. Sacagawea may be only fifteen, but she is as hardy as any warrior. She won't slow you down, with or without a baby on her back."

Meriwether didn't doubt that for a moment. From what he had seen of the Indian women, they were as courageous and spirited as the men. One of the Mandan women's jobs was to paddle round "bullboats" across the Missouri River. It astonished Meriwether to see them set out when the water was so choppy that he would have instructed his own men not to go. The women were also the beasts of burden for their husbands. In fact, just the day before, Chief Big White had come to visit the fort, bringing a hundred pounds of meat with him, all of it carried in a bundle tied to his wife's back.

Later that week Charbonneau and his two wives moved inside the walls of Fort Mandan.

A week after that a Mandan warrior came to tell Meriwether that a party of Sioux and Arikara Indians had attacked five Mandan hunters. They had left one man dead, wounded two others, and stolen nine horses. Meriwether sighed when he heard the news. It had taken so little time for the Arikaras to break their promise of peace with their neighbors. For a moment he caught a glimpse of the difficulties that lay ahead for the United States government as it tried to create peace among tribes who had been warring for generations. In fact, Meriwether hated to admit it, but the Plains Indians' entire way of life, from the manner in which they chose a chief to their dances and religious ceremonies, all seemed to be based on raids and wars. It was going to take a lot more than an army captain's urging for them to be willing to seek a permanent peace.

In early December Chief Big White informed Meriwether that a herd of buffalo had been spotted not far from the village. He invited the Corps of Discovery to join them in a buffalo hunt and offered to lend them horses for the occasion. It was just the diversion the men needed, and the meat would be a welcome supplement to their food supply.

Meriwether enjoyed every minute of the hunt and came away with new admiration for the Mandan warriors. The warriors rode bareback at hair-raising speeds, clinging to the horse with their knees as they aimed their bows and arrows. Even with guns and bullets, Meriwether's men killed nowhere near as many buffalo as the Mandan.

The women ran along behind the horses, butchering the huge animals before wolves moved in for a feast.

The next day, as Meriwether walked around Chief Big White's village, he saw a flurry of activity. It seemed as though everyone was involved in doing something with the butchered buffalo. Groups of women were twisting buffalo hair into rope while others were pounding brains into a paste that was smeared on a hide to tan it. Warriors were busy carving bones into knives and arrowheads, and a group of young girls were tending a pot of buffalo hooves that were being boiled down and made into glue.

Both the tribe and the Corps of Discovery dined on buffalo for weeks, first as fresh meat, then in the form of jerky. However, by the end of January the corps was running out of meat, and their other food supplies were also dwindling. Something had to be done. Ironically it was not the expedition's hunters who came to the rescue but Private John Shields, their blacksmith. Up to this time Shields had been busy trading his skills for food for the corps. He had done everything from mending iron hoes and rifles to sharpening axes. But now there was nothing more to do. However, in his time with the Mandan Shields had noticed that the warriors prized a particular type of battle-axe, one that he could easily make in his blacksmith shop. He drew a pattern and set to work melting down the keelboat's iron stove and fashioning it into battle-axes. The Indians traded the finished axes for bags of corn, which fed the men through the rest of the winter.

Most of the men in the Corps of Discovery had never experienced such cold as they did that winter. Icy winds whipped across the Great Plains and piled up drifts of snow against Fort Mandan. Twice a day Meriwether recorded the outside temperature in his journal. He also recorded in his journal the birth of the youngest member of the group that would travel west in the spring. It was the first birth he had ever helped with, and on the night of February 11, 1805, in the light of a flickering candle, he wrote, "About five o'clock this evening to one of the wives of Charbonneau was delivered a fine boy." He went on to tell how he had used an ancient Indian method of speeding up the delivery, having the mother-to-be swallow some of the crushed rattle of a rattlesnake. Whether this helped or not, Meriwether could not say, but soon afterward Sacagewea gave birth to Jean Baptiste Charbonneau, a very French name for a little brown baby with jet black eyes. Little Jean Baptiste was an instant hit with the men. Soon William had nicknamed him Pomp, a name that stuck.

Toward the end of March, large chunks of ice and debris came floating down the river along with drowned buffalo that had been caught on the ice as it broke up. The Mandan warriors jumped nimbly from one chunk of ice to the next, tying ropes to the carcasses of the buffalo and dragging them ashore. Once again there was meat for everyone to eat.

As soon as the ice chunks melted, Meriwether wanted the Corps of Discovery to be on its way. He and William had worked hard all winter, writing fuller accounts of what they had seen so far, supervising the making of six thirty-foot-long dugout canoes, and repacking the keelboat for the return trip to St. Louis.

Finally, on April 7, 1805, Meriwether Lewis stood on a bluff overlooking the river, and Scannon stood beside him, wagging his tail and barking. On the river below were nine boats. Two canoes and the keelboat were on their way downstream to St. Louis. On board were reports and letters, a collection of sixty-eight mineral specimens Meriwether had collected and labeled, and hundreds of plant samples, including a root the Indians said cured rabies. Meriwether was sure that President Jefferson would pass the root on to Dr. Rush. Stuffed animals and their bones were also aboard the boats. Meriwether had even included some live animals—four magpies, a prairie dog, and a grouse hen. He smiled as he thought of Jefferson trying to corral the prairie dog!

Corporal Richard Warfington had been put in charge of the group going back. With them was Joseph Gravelines, who would serve as interpreter. Meriwether hoped that Corporal Warfington would be able to safely guide the keelboat past the hostile Sioux. It was a gamble, but Warfington had been given instructions to fight to the death if necessary. At all costs, the precious cargo of the keelboat and canoes had to get through.

Traveling upstream in the opposite direction from the keelboat were the six newly hewn dugout canoes and the two pirogues that Meriwether would catch up to. On board the canoes and pirogues were William Clark, three sergeants, twenty-four privates, two French interpreters, an Indian girl and her seven-week-old baby, and a black slave. It was more than the fifteen men Meriwether and Jefferson had envisaged going on the trip. But after traveling on the river for more than a year, Meriwether realized that the original estimate for the size of the group had been inadequate.

The plan was to leave the cumbersome pirogues at the bottom of the Great Falls of the Missouri River and portage the dugouts around the falls. Hidatsa horsemen, who had seen the falls during their raids on tribes to the west, had told Meriwether about them. At the top of the falls the Corps of Discovery would assemble the iron frame canoe made back in Harpers Ferry and stretch hides over it. If all went well, the canoe would be able to carry most of the provisions now loaded in the pirogues.

Meriwether watched as the men heaved on the paddles against the current. The white pirogue led the fleet. Since it was the most stable vessel, it carried Meriwether's astronomical instruments, medicines, gunpowder, and writing equipment. Sacagawea sat near the bow of the craft, Pomp strapped to a board on her back. Her husband sat behind them with George Drouillard. Six privates sat at the sides and dipped their paddles rhythmically into the water. Three of the soldiers were the nonswimmers of the corps, and William Clark had assigned them to the pirogue in the hope it would not capsize.

The sun glistened on the water as Meriwether watched the boats slip from sight and off the edge of the map into Terra Incognita.

Chapter 13

A Fork in the River

The canoes and pirogues sped along, sometimes covering as much as twenty-three miles a day, twice the daily distance the corps had made with the keelboat. Spread out on both sides of the river was an endless grassy plain. On it roamed thousands of buffalo, elk, and antelope. The buffalo were so tame that they would wander into camp at night. Some mornings the men had to throw sticks and stones at them to chase them away.

With so many animals around, they always had plenty of food. Flocks of geese en route to their nesting grounds flew in formation overhead, and the men loved to fire at them from the canoes and watch as Scannon leapt into the river to retrieve the dead birds. Sacagawea collected an array of various roots to cook that were a welcome addition to the corps' nearly all-meat diet.

On April 13 Meriwether spotted the tracks of a huge bear by the water's edge. He felt sure it was the infamous grizzly bear that the Mandan and Hidatsa warriors had spoken about. The warriors feared the animal like no other. They told Meriwether that even when ten men attacked one of these bears, chances were that one of them would lose his life. In preparation for a bear hunt, the men performed the same religious ceremonies as they did when they went to battle.

Meriwether was sure the Indians were exaggerating, making their bear hunts sound more daring than they were. In his opinion, the Corps of Discovery did not need to worry about grizzly bears as long as they had their guns loaded and ready to fire.

After sighting more bear tracks, Meriwether finally got to encounter a grizzly. It was April 29, three days after they passed the mouth of the Yellowstone River, and Meriwether and John Potts were walking along the water's edge. Suddenly Potts let out a yell. "Two bears!"

Meriwether spun around, his hands instinctively reaching for his rifle. There behind them were two bears, weighing about three hundred pounds each, lumbering through some bushes at the water's edge.

"I'll take the one on the left," Meriwether said.

Potts raised his rifle to his shoulder and fired. *Bang.* The bear fell to the ground and lay there.

Meriwether raised his rifle and squeezed the trigger. The second grizzly roared and fell to the ground. Moments later, blood spurting from its right shoulder, the bear scrambled up again. It lumbered toward Meriwether and Potts. Quickly the two men poured gunpowder into their rifles, tampered it, and rolled a ball of shot down the barrel. The bear was closing on them fast as they raised their rifles. Two shots rang out, and the animal fell down dead.

That night Meriwether wrote in his journal about killing the grizzly bears. "It is a much more furious and formidable anamal, and will frequently pursue the hunter when wounded. It is asstonishing to see the wounds they will bear before they can be put to death. The Indians may well fear this anamal equiped as they generally are with their bows and arrows or indifferent fuzees [poor quality guns] but in the hands of skillfull riflemen they are by no means as formidable or dangerous as they have been represented."

Meriwether would soon take these words back! On May 11 he was on the front pirogue when he heard gunshots. He swung around and noted that the two canoes bringing up the rear were missing. Quickly he ordered the pirogue to turn around and head downstream. Adrenaline pumped through his body. He held his rifle ready. What would he find around the bend in the river? Had Indians attacked?

More shots rang out as the pirogue rounded the bend. Meriwether scanned the shore. He saw one canoe pulled up on the beach, while the second was in the middle of the river with two men in it. Next he heard a shout and looked up to see two of his men leaping off a twenty-foot-high cliff into the water below. To his horror, a huge grizzly bear plunged off the cliff after them. Hitting the water, it looked around and swam toward the men.

Another man appeared on the bank and fired his rifle at the bear. The creature flailed in the water for a moment and then was still.

Meriwether ordered the pirogue to come along-side the bear, and when he was convinced the bear was dead, one of the men tied a rope around its leg and they dragged it ashore.

Once the bear was on the beach, Meriwether learned what had happened. The six men in the rear canoes had spotted the bear and come up with a plan to kill it. They would sneak up on the bear, and four of them would fire at it while the other two men kept their rifles in reserve in case anything went wrong. Their plan did go wrong. All four shots hit the bear, but instead of dying, the bear became enraged and attacked the men. Two of them escaped in one of the canoes, and the other four found refuge in some willow trees. From there they fired at the bear several more times, but the bear managed to knock two of the men out of the tree, and the men fled for their lives, throwing away their unloaded guns and powder pouches. They then threw themselves over the cliff just as Meriwether rounded the bend in the river and saw what happened next.

Meriwether measured the bear. Its feet were nine inches across and thirteen inches in length, with claws that were seven inches long. The claws could shred a man to pieces in seconds. Meriwether estimated the animal weighed about six hundred pounds, though he had no scale large enough to weigh it. When the bear was butchered, they discovered that eight bullets had hit it. When it plunged over the cliff, its shoulder had already been shattered by one bullet, and four had passed right through its lungs.

Meriwether quickly revised his conclusion about the grizzly bears. He would rather meet two armed Indians than another adult grizzly. He ordered the men to leave the bears alone unless they were being a nuisance or were set to attack. The men nodded their heads in instant agreement.

The day was not yet over, however, and more drama awaited them. Meriwether and William were walking along the edge of the river at about 4 P.M. when some stiff gusts of wind blew up. The white pirogue was on the far side of the river, where the men were using a small square sail to power the boat upstream. One of the powerful gusts of wind caught the pirogue and turned it sideways to the wind, and it began to list precariously. Charbonneau, who was steering the boat, panicked, fearing it would capsize and throw him into the water, where he would drown. Instead of pulling the tiller and heading the pirogue into the wind where it would right itself, he began to wail and cry out to God for mercy. All the while the pirogue was filling with water.

Cruzatte called to Charbonneau to grab the tiller and turn the boat, but Charbonneau would not listen, at least not until Cruzatte threatened to shoot him if he didn't do as asked. Finally Charbonneau grabbed the tiller, and slowly the boat turned into the wind and righted itself, not, however, before it had filled with water to within one inch of the gunwales. By now important reports Meriwether had written and specimens he had collected were bobbing in the water. Onshore Meriwether was beside himself. He could scarcely believe what he was seeing. His life's work was floating away!

While the men furiously began bailing the pirogue to stop it from completely sinking, Sacagawea sprang into action. She began crawling about the half-sunken boat, reaching out and scooping up the items that had been washed overboard. All the while she carefully made sure Pomp's head stayed clear of the water so he did not drown and make the disaster worse than it already was.

Finally the pirogue was brought to shore, and although everything in it was wet, including Meriwether's navigational equipment, thanks to Sacagewea's quick thinking, nothing important was lost. Relieved, that night Meriwether handed out an extra ration of whiskey to the men, even Charbonneau, whom William described as "perhaps the most timid waterman in the world."

Meriwether was so impressed by the Indian girl's quick thinking in saving the items that had washed overboard that he named the next river they passed Sacagawea River in her honor.

Although the Hidatsa warriors had told Meriwether about the upper reaches of the Missouri River, Meriwether was taken by surprise when on June 2, two days after entering an area where the river flowed between high white cliffs, the expedition came to a fork. One branch of the river flowed northwest and the other southwest. Only one branch was the Missouri River, which would take them to the foot of the Rocky Mountains. But which one? The Hidatsa warriors who had told Meriwether about the upper reaches of the Missouri River had not told him about the fork because they had taken a shortcut overland and so were unaware that the fork even existed. But now the Corps of Discovery was at the fork, and Meriwether and William were dumbfounded as to which branch they should follow. To pick the wrong fork could mean the end of the expedition.

The group set up camp beside the river for the night while the two co-captains discussed what to do. Meriwether took readings from the stars, and William recorded them by candlelight. They hoped that plotting their position would give them some guidance as to which fork to choose, but it didn't. As soon as the sun came up, Meriwether measured the width of the right-hand fork, which seemed to flow in a more direct line from the west. The fork was two hundred yards wide, and the water was deep, tepid, slow moving and thick with sediment. It also had a muddy bottom.

In contrast, the left fork was 372 yards wide and flowed from the southwest. It was shallower than the other fork, but its current flowed more swiftly. As well, its water was crystal clear and flowed over smooth rocks.

There was little disagreement over which fork was the continuation of the Missouri River. Every person on the expedition bar two, from the trappers to Sacagawea, was convinced it was the right-hand fork that flowed from the west. Only Meriwether and William disagreed. They both had a hunch that the left fork was the Missouri, despite the fact that it headed in a more southerly direction. But unwilling to move forward on a hunch, they decided to explore up both rivers.

Meriwether slung a knapsack on his back and headed off with a team of six men up the right-hand fork. Meanwhile, William took a group and went to explore the left fork. Two days and sixty miles later, Meriwether was convinced he was not traveling up the Missouri River, while the other six men were sure they were. They arrived back at camp exhausted and covered with sores from numerous encounters with prickly pear. William got back to camp ahead of Meriwether, and he too stuck to the notion that the left fork was the Missouri, although he had not found the Great Falls. He and Meriwether were sure the clear water bubbling down the river came from the mountains, while the river with the muddy sediment most likely wound its way around the plains for some distance.

The following morning the two co-captains called a meeting to explain to the men that the expedition would follow the left fork that headed to the southwest. Meriwether named the other fork the Marias River after his cousin in Virginia. None of the men wasted a moment complaining about their captains' decision, even though they all disagreed with it.

Before they started out again, Meriwether and William made another decision. The water flowed much faster after the fork, and they needed to lighten the load in the boats. They instructed the men to dig two large holes on an island in the mouth of the Marias River. Into the holes were placed the blacksmith's bellows, kegs of salt pork, beaver traps, and gunpowder—all supplies the co-captains did not want to carry over the mountains. If for some reason they came back this way, there would be food and supplies waiting for them.

The men also hid one of the pirogues in a thicket. With fewer supplies to transport, they no longer needed as many boats.

On June 10 they set off upriver again. William took charge of the boats while Meriwether hand-picked four men to set out overland with him in search of the Great Falls. If they were following the correct fork in the river, they should find the falls before too long.

Meriwether and his men followed the river for two days. On the third day Meriwether began to despair of ever finding the falls. Late that afternoon, however, he heard a faint rumble that began to grow in intensity with each step he took. And then he saw the spray rising into the air like smoke. He had found the Great Falls of the Missouri River.

That night Meriwether and his men camped at the bottom of the falls. Over a campfire they cooked buffalo meat and cutthroat trout. Everything was going according to plan, and the next morning Meriwether sent Private Joseph Field back downriver to tell William they had found the falls. The other three men set to work drying buffalo meat and catching fish while Meriwether took Scannon with him and walked upstream to the end of the falls.

The falls were spectacular, unlike anything Meriwether had seen before, and he had a hard time taking his eyes off them to concentrate on where he was walking. Sometimes he walked on the bluff overlooking the tumbling water, and other times he scrambled along the rocky shoreline, clambering up and over huge rocks as he went. Over a five-mile stretch the river fell about forty feet. And as it did so, it threw cascades of misty spray into the air. In turn, the spray broke the rays of the sun into a dazzling array of colors.

At what he supposed to be the head of the falls, Meriwether sat on a rock and peered back down the falls. The Hidatsa warriors had said it would take about half a day to portage around the falls. Given the challenging climb, Meriwether estimated it would probably take the Corps of Discovery a day to haul their canoes to the top of the falls.

As he sat taking in the view and listening to the roar of the water, Meriwether began to notice something strange. The roar of the water was not just coming from below him. Farther upriver he could hear more water falling. Surely there weren't more falls upstream. The Hidatsa warriors had said nothing about them. Surely they would have told him if there were more falls. He was probably just hearing an echo.

Still, being an explorer, Meriwether picked up his rifle, whistled for Scannon to follow, and headed farther upstream just to be sure. As he rounded a bend, his heart sank. Right before him was another waterfall, about twenty feet high. He scrambled up it, only to find another waterfall, and then another. Finally he reached a place where the river was smooth and wide, and the land was once again flat. This was the head of the Great Falls of the Missouri River. Despite what the Hidatsa warriors had told him, the falls stretched on for twelve miles and consisted of five separate waterfalls. In all, the river dropped 412 feet from the beginning to the end of the falls. It was a formidable obstacle, and Meriwether wondered how they were ever going to lug the canoes and their supplies to the top of the falls.

Chapter 14

A Happy Reunion

Two days after first sighting the falls, Meriwether, along with William and the Corps of Discovery, was camped on the south bank of the Missouri River six miles below. He had no choice but to find a way to get the men, canoes, and their supplies around the falls.

After discussing it, Meriwether and William decided not to directly follow the rugged riverbank past the falls. Instead they would look for an easier path to the head of the falls by going inland a little from the river's edge.

William set out with a small party of men to find the best route. While they were gone Meriwether supervised the rest of the men. They had much work to do. Since the remaining pirogue was too heavy to carry, it was emptied and hidden in some bushes. The other canoes were emptied, and everything was dried and repacked for the portage. Patrick Gass, the corps's best carpenter, and three other men set to work making wheels from the trunks of cottonwood trees and axles from the pirogue's mast. These would be fitted under the canoes so that they could be pulled along on a rope.

In the evenings the men sat around the campfire and sewed new moccasins from buffalo hides. They reinforced them with two soles because the plains were thick with prickly pear and the huge buffalo herds had left the ground so churned up that walking on it soon bruised the men's feet.

Everyone worked hard except Sacagawea, who lay near death from an infection. Pomp crawled around his mother and among the men as they worked. Meriwether worried constantly about Sacagawea and treated her with poultices and tree bark. Thankfully, by the time William returned to camp on June 21, Sacagawea was well on the way to recovery.

William reported the good news that he had found a passable route to the head of the Great Falls. Unfortunately, the route was eighteen miles long and infested with wolves, rattlesnakes, grizzly bears, and mosquitoes.

Dangerous animals notwithstanding, the men started on the portage the next morning. The first canoe was heaved up onto the wooden axles and loaded with the iron frame for the new canoe and the necessary tools to put it together. The loaded canoe weighed well over two thousand pounds. The plan was for all but two of the men and Sacagawea and Pomp to make the first portage. Meriwether and three men would then stay at the head of the falls and assemble the iron frame for the new canoe, which they would use in place of the pirogue. They would also shoot buffalo, whose meat could be dried for the long journey over the mountains.

It was a crystal clear morning when they set out. The sun glistened on the distant snow-capped mountains, and meadowlarks sang. However, the men had little time to appreciate the unspoiled beauty of far-off mountains. Their eyes were on each step they took. Prickly pear thorns soon ripped through their moccasins. Some men's hands began to bleed from pulling on the rope, others twisted ankles, and one man even dislocated his shoulder. Meriwether jerked it back into place, and the men pushed on. Every yard they covered was a hard-fought victory. The axles broke and new ones had to be made. Finally just before nightfall they reached the head of the falls. A number of the men were so exhausted from the portage that they fell down where they stood and went to sleep. Scannon patrolled throughout the night, barking at grizzly bears when they came too close to the men.

The following day, William and the rest of the men, except Meriwether, Patrick Gass, Joseph Field, and John Shields, limped back to base camp to get another canoe and load of equipment.

Meriwether and the other three began fitting the iron frame together. The men quickly dubbed the new canoe Experiment because they had never seen anything like it before. Meriwether could hardly contain his excitement as the boat he had designed began to take shape.

Every second night the portage crew hobbled to the top of the falls with another canoe in tow. One night William pulled seventeen thorns out of his blistered feet. Other men had huge welts on their bodies from infected mosquito bites. One evening the men staggered in bruised and bleeding. They had been caught in a violent storm far from cover and were pelted with enormous hailstones.

By June 30 they had only one more canoe to portage, and the preparation of Experiment was nearing an end. Twenty-eight elk skins and four buffalo hides had been tanned, cut, and sewn together to cover the canoe. There was just one problem. Meriwether had intended to seal the seams and make the skins watertight by painting them with tar—tar that came from pine tree sap. Alas, there were no pine trees on the high plains, and Meriwether had to experiment with a mixture of bear fat and charcoal as a substitute. He had no idea whether or not it would work; only time would tell.

The Fourth of July was a busy day for the men. Everything was now finally portaged to the head of the falls and packed back into the canoes, except for Experiment. The iron-framed canoe hung over the fire so that the hides could dry in preparation for sealing the seams. To celebrate the day, Meriwether dispensed the last of the whiskey to the men, who danced to Pierre Cruzatte's fiddle playing until a thunderstorm broke up the party at nine o'clock.

By now everyone was eager to get back into the boats and start moving again. It was still a long way to the Pacific Coast, and the majestic mountain peaks in the distance that shone in the early morning sun had to be crossed to get to their destination. They couldn't afford to spend too many summer days camped by the river.

The hides on the iron-frame canoe seemed to take forever to dry, despite the fire that was constantly tended under them. Finally, on July 9, it was time to paint the seams of Experiment with the substitute tar mixture and launch her. Meriwether breathed a sigh of relief as the canoe bobbed up and down in the water. The boat was steady, even when loaded with supplies. But just as the expedition was ready to set out again, a fierce storm swept in from the plains. Meriwether quickly ordered the canoes unpacked, and they waited for the torrential rain to stop. When it did, Experiment lay at the bottom of the river.

Meriwether was devastated. He ordered the boat pulled up on to the beach and examined it. Sure enough, the bear grease and charcoal "tar" had not been tough enough to seal the seams, which still gaped open, allowing water to pour in. Meriwether's body slumped when he thought of the time and effort in Harpers Ferry perfecting the design and getting it built and the energy used to lug the frame mile after mile upriver. It had all been for nothing. Experiment was not fit to paddle, and without the proper tar it never would be.

Meriwether was so distraught he hardly noticed when William took charge and ordered the men to find cottonwood trees large enough to hew into more dugout canoes. Five days passed before the new canoes were loaded and ready to go. Precious time had been lost, and Meriwether became increasingly worried about the trek over the mountains. According to the Hidatsa Indians, it would take only half a day to traverse the mountains, but after his experience with the falls, Meriwether doubted that estimate. And without horses to help carry their supplies, it might be impossible to cross them at all. The only way to get horses now was to find the Shoshone Indians.

As they traveled on upriver above the falls, the scenery began to change. Gone were the wide-open plains and the vast herds of buffalo, replaced by jagged rocks and glimpses of fleet-footed mountain sheep. It became more difficult for the hunters to catch their daily quota of game, especially since Meriwether was anxious about every shot they fired. What if a Shoshone scout heard a shot and thought it was an enemy invasion?

Hard days of pushing, pulling, poling, and paddling the canoes melded together as the men struggled upriver through valleys that sweltered in the summer heat. The men felt lucky when they covered eighteen miles in a day.

By the time they reached Three Forks on July 27, the men were almost too exhausted to go on. But as exhausted as he was, Meriwether was relieved. It meant they were getting very close to Shoshone territory.

Thinking that the three rivers that came together at that spot deserved grand names, Meriwether named them the Gallitin, Madison, and Jefferson Rivers, in honor of the secretary of the treasury, the secretary of state, and, of course, the president himself.

The Corps of Discovery camped at Three Forks for two days. The men rested, hunted, fished, and mended their tattered buckskin clothes. Meriwether also fixed the latitude and longitude of the point where the forks met. With that task accomplished, the expedition continued up the Jefferson River, which was the fork that branched off to the right.

Two days later Sacagawea cheered everyone up with her announcement that she recognized a rocky outcrop. She told them it was right at the spot where Hidatsa warriors had kidnapped her. They were now in Shoshone territory. From then on, each day a small group of men marched on ahead of the canoes. Their job was to look for any sign of Indians. However, fewer and fewer men were up to the rigors of such a march. William had a tumor on his ankle that made it impossible for him to walk more than a few feet, and Toussaint Charbonneau, Patrick Gass, and five of the privates spent hours lying in the canoes with ailments ranging from acute diarrhea to infected blisters. In fact, no one was particularly well, and the increasing scarcity of fresh meat did not allow the men to build up their strength. With each passing day, Meriwether became more alarmed about the state of the men's health. He wondered whether they would all make it to the mountains, let alone over them.

When the Jefferson River forked, they followed the branch that veered southwest. They named the other fork the Wisdom River. As they continued on upriver, they had still not sighted any Shoshone Indians, and Meriwether was beginning to worry. The men were weak, and they needed horses desperately if they were to make it over the mountains to the Columbia River.

On August 8, Meriwether chose three men, George Drouillard, John Shields, and Hugh McNeal, who set out with him on foot. Their mission was to find horses and bring them back, even if it meant crossing the mountains and making contact with Indians on the other side.

The men trekked across stony, broken ground that in places gave way to swamp, where small rivers and streams took meandering twists and turns, and up into a pass that they later learned the Indians called Lemhi Pass. It was there that they caught their first glimpse of a Shoshone warrior on horseback. Meriwether quickly unfolded his blanket and spread it on the ground. He hoped the Indian would see it as a gesture of friendship. Apparently he did not, because the warrior turned his horse and galloped off.

All four men stood silent as they watched the horse and rider disappear. What would happen now that they had been spotted? Would a raiding party come and kill them or take them prisoner?

No one slept much that night, or the following one. Meriwether was torn between the desire to sight another Shoshone Indian and anxiety at what might happen if they did.

On August 12 the four weary travelers climbed higher into the mountains. They followed a tiny stream that eventually ran out as they neared the top of a ridge. Once at the top of the ridge, Meriwether looked out over range after range of steep mountains. His heart dropped. The mountains seemed to go on forever!

Nearby another stream started, but this time it flowed west instead of east. Meriwether realized it could mean only one thing—they had reached the Continental Divide. All streams to the east eventually found their way to the Atlantic Ocean, while those on the west side of the ridge emptied into the Pacific. Meriwether took one step down the western side of the ridge, and with it he stepped out of Louisiana, the United States' latest acquisition, and into unclaimed Oregon country.

The other three men stood and marveled for a few moments at the sea of mountains stretched out before them and then followed Meriwether down the steep western slope. Not far down, they found a rough Indian track and followed it until they made camp for the night. The following day they hiked on, desperately looking for some sign of Indians.

It was about midday when they rounded a bend in the track, and there only thirty yards in front of them were three Indians—two girls and an old woman. Meriwether thought fast. He had to show the woman they did not mean her and the girls any harm. He bent down and laid his rifle on the ground, telling his men to do the same. Then alone and very slowly, he began to approach the women. The older girl dropped her basket and ran away, but the old woman and the younger girl clung to each other, terror etched on their faces.

After months in the sun, Meriwether was so tanned he feared the woman might mistake him for an Indian, so he rolled up his sleeves to show his natural color. When he reached the woman, she was shaking with fear. He smiled and took some beads from his knapsack. He handed them to her and instructed Drouillard to use sign language to tell the woman the beads were a gift. This appeared to calm the old Indian, and soon both she and the girl were happily examining a mirror also handed over.

Drouillard managed to communicate to the woman that they wanted to speak to her chief, and she motioned for the men to follow her. They all set off down the track.

Two miles farther they heard the thunder of horse hooves as sixty painted warriors galloped over a hill. The warriors swooped down on the men, their feathered warbonnets streaming behind them, bows and arrows poised for action.

The warriors halted fifty yards from the men. The old woman walked toward the horses. Meriwether saw his opportunity. Trying hard to look calm, he laid his rifle on the ground, pulled out an American flag, and began to follow the woman. He hoped this tactic would work. If it didn't, he and his men could be surrounded and shot within seconds.

The old woman started talking and pointing at Meriwether and the other men. Then she held out the beads she had been given. The warrior on the lead horse, whom Meriwether assumed was the chief, jumped down from his mount and walked toward the men. He stopped in front of Meriwether, put his hands on Meriwether's shoulders, and pressed his cheek against Meriwether's. The tension was broken. The chief accepted that the men had come in peace.

Soon other warriors joined in the greeting, and before long all four white men's faces were smeared with warpaint and grease. They all proceeded down to the village, where Meriwether and the chief, whose name turned out to be Cameahwait, smoked a peace pipe and communicated as best they could through Drouillard's handsigns. Meriwether learned that the Indians had run out of food and were preparing to head over the great divide to go buffalo hunting with other Shoshone and Flathead Indians.

Now Meriwether really had a problem. Somehow he had to convince Chief Camcahwait to help him get the rest of the expedition to the village and then trade horses from the Indians so they could continue over the rugged terrain to the ocean. He wished he had Sacagawea with him. It would make communication so much easier.

It took some time, but eventually Meriwether was able to convince Chief Cameahwait to go back with him and rendezvous with William and the rest of the expedition.

Early on August 15 sixteen Indians left the village with the white men. By now everyone was very hungry, as neither group had much food. At lunch that day, the men's supplies, which amounted to one pound of flour, were cooked into a dumpling and quickly eaten.

The following morning, Drouillard and Shields were able to track down and kill a deer. When the Shoshone Indians saw the dead animal, they leapt off their horses and ran to it. Without a moment's hesitation, they began ripping the carcass apart, pulling off chunks of meat and eating them raw. Blood dripped from their mouths as they stuffed the food in. Meriwether felt both repulsion and pity. He was repulsed by the way the Shoshone were eating, yet he pitied them being so hungry that they were prepared to gulp down uncooked meat.

Two more deer and a pronghorn antelope were killed that day, and everyone lay down to sleep that night with a full stomach. This time the meat was cooked before it was eaten!

At four o'clock the following day Meriwether spotted the rest of the Corps of Discovery. It was a happy reunion. Meriwether had returned with horses just as he promised he would. And now that the Corps had been reunited, Sacagawea would be able to translate for him. Meriwether sent one of the men to get her.

Sacagawea, with Pomp bound securely to her back, made her way over to where Meriwether and Chief Cameahwait were standing. As she took a close look at Cameahwait, she let out a scream, then ran to the chief and threw her arms around him. Crying and laughing at the same time, Sacagawea spoke to her husband, Toussaint Charbonneau. Quickly Charbonneau translated her words into French, and Private Francis Labiche translated them for Meriwether. "The chief is the brother of Sacagawea!" he announced.

It was amazing but true. A sister who had long been considered dead was united with her brother. Meriwether could not have been happier. Now he knew he would get the help the Corps of Discovery needed in getting to the Columbia River.

Things fell into place after the reunion of brother and sister. Cameahwait explained to Meriwether that the Shoshone were at a severe disadvantage because the Spanish, who previously controlled the region, would not trade guns with the Indians. Because of this, the Shoshone had only three old guns, whereas their enemies on the plains had many guns they had traded from the British and the French. That is why the Shoshone were starving. They put their lives at risk every time they went down onto the plains to hunt among the well-armed tribes.

Meriwether promised the chief that gun traders would soon be following and his tribe would have all the guns they wanted. He then moved on to another subject. Meriwether wanted to know what Chief Cameahwait knew of the area beyond the mountains. Cameahwait talked of a stream near their village in the mountains. "I understand from an Indian who inhabits the river below the rocky mountains that it runs a great way toward the setting sun and finally loses itself in a great lake of water which is illy tasting," he said.

"Illy tasting" could mean only one thing: It was salty! The stream ran all the way to the Pacific Ocean.

Meriwether also learned that there was an elderly Shoshone man back at the village who, according to Chief Cameahwait, had been all the way over the mountains to the tribe who lived on the other side. The chief suggested the man might be willing to guide the expedition to their village.

This was almost too much good fortune for Meriwether and William to take in, and they named the place they were camped Camp Fortunate.

Both men were eager to be on their way over the mountains as soon as possible.

Chapter 15

A Holler of Delight

It was September 1, 1805, before the Corps of Discovery was ready to move again. In the two weeks previous, the men had stashed their canoes and some provisions in case they were needed again and, with the help of the Shoshones, transferred their luggage and supplies up to the Indians' camp. Once at camp, they traded for thirty horses, but the Shoshone drove a hard bargain, costing the corps musket balls, knives, and even William Clark's pistol. It seemed family connections went only so far!

Frost lay thick on the ground on the day they set out. The old Shoshone man who had been all the way over the mountains agreed to be their guide. The men nicknamed him "Old Toby," and he led them north out of the village. They would not be following the stream Chief Cameahwait had told them about that led to the illy tasting water. The chief insisted there was no way to canoe down the stream or hike along its banks. Indeed, William had tried to do this himself, only to find what Chief Cameahwait said was right. The corps would have to follow where Old Toby led them.

At first the track wound through stony hill country and then petered out, leaving the men to hack their way through thickets of balsam fir. As the men moved north, the stony sloping hills gave way to rugged mountains. Men and horses slipped and fell as they climbed toward a flat area Old Toby told them was the pass through the mountains they would follow. Old Toby predicted that if they followed the pass, in ten days they would come to the west-flowing river, and five days on down the river they would find the saltwater "lake" they sought.

Despite Old Toby's prediction of soon reaching their destination, the journey was grueling as the corps struggled on into the mountains. Icy sleet driven by the wind whipped around their buckskin clothing, sapping their flagging strength. All they had to eat to renew their strength was portable soup and the occasional grouse someone shot. Meriwether was eager to get to the other side of the mountains, where he assumed there would be an adequate food supply. He found himself having to reevaluate this expectation when on September 4 the corps met up with a band of four hundred friendly Salish Indians.

The Salish were in terrible condition, gnawing the bark off trees and scavenging for roots. The band had a Shoshone boy with them, and so through one more link in the chain of interpreters, Meriwether was able to gain information from them. They were on their way over the mountains to meet up with the Shoshone for a buffalo hunt. They had no food with them but had over five hundred horses, which they hoped to trade and use for the hunt. Meriwether took the opportunity to trade out some of his worst horses, and when the groups parted, the Corps of Discovery had thirty-nine horses, three colts, and one mule.

Finally they reached Lolo Pass and crossed the Continental Divide. With one range of mountains behind them, the corps descended into a long valley. The going then got easier, and instead of covering five miles a day as they had on the way up the mountain, the men were now able to cover up to twenty-one miles a day. However, as they followed Old Toby on through the mountains, their supply of food started to get desperately short. The men began to kill and eat the colts one at a time, and they even ate a crow one of the men had shot.

Hunger was not their only problem. The packhorse loaded with their spare winter clothing strayed and was never found. As well, men and horses tumbled down the steep, slippery mountainside, and Old Toby got lost, causing the expedition to retrace its steps until it picked up the trail again. Then on September 16, wet snow began to fall, leaving slushy puddles of dirty water along the trail. Meriwether melted some of the snow and boiled horsemeat in it to make soup.

By the next day, Meriwether and William realized they had to do something. The men were still willing to follow them on through the mountains, but given the conditions, they were getting weaker by the hour. The Corps of Discovery could not go on much farther without food.

There was only one solution to their situation. The expedition would have to split up. William would lead a group that would ride ahead and scout for food. Neither Meriwether nor William liked the idea of splitting up under such dangerous conditions, but they had no alternative.

As soon as the sun rose on September 18, William and seven other men mounted horses and waved farewell to the rest of the Corps of Discovery.

After six grueling days on the trail, Meriwether and the rest of the expedition caught up to Reuben Field, who was waiting for them with good news. William and the other men had reached the Nez Perce Indians, who were camped a few miles away. Field unwrapped a package of roots and dried fish that the Indians had given him and distributed the food among the starving members of the expedition.

With a little food in their stomachs and hope in their hearts, the men pushed on the last seven miles to the Indian village. That night the men, along with Sacagawea and Pomp, sat around the campfire. It was a bright moonlit night, and as he turned to look behind him, Meriwether could see the outline of the Rocky Mountains. He was not sure how they had done it, but somehow the Corps of Discovery had made it safely over them to the home of the Nez Perce Indians, who made the western side of the mountains their home.

The complete change of diet the men experienced among the Nez Perce, from virtually all meat to camas roots and dried fish, was volatile. Every member of the corps got sick, and Meriwether was the sickest of all. Alternating bouts of vomiting and diarrhea left him feeling weak and barely able to stand. The other men recovered faster than he did, and they set to work making dugout canoes for the trip downriver to the sea.

Two weeks passed before the canoes were finished and everyone was well enough to travel. Finally, on October 7, 1805, the Corps of Discovery set out again. They left their horses for the Nez Perce to look after and headed out of camp guided by Chief Twisted Hair, who along with Old Toby had agreed to accompany them part of the way to the coast.

The river that flowed through Nez Perce territory was swift with many bubbling rapids. This time the men had no complaints about the current because for the first time since leaving Camp Wood, seventeen months before, they were paddling with the current and not against it. The canoes smashed headlong into massive waves, crashed over boulders, and were tossed about in the churning water of the river. In the process, men and equipment were pitched overboard. The men were recovered, but most of the tomahawks, shot pouches, bedding, and clothing were not. The items were either swept away or left at the bottom of the turbulent river. Normally Meriwether and William would have ordered the canoes be portaged around such rapids, but autumn had already settled over the area, and they were willing to take whatever risks necessary to make it to the Pacific Ocean before winter overtook them.

After running fifteen rapids in one day, Old Toby climbed out of a canoe with terror etched on his face. He waded from the river and ran into some nearby bushes. No one could find him, and Meriwether concluded that he was so scared by the rapids he had started for home, alone and without his pay!

The rivers on this side of the mountains certainly were different from the Missouri. On the eastern side of the mountains, the men had gone for weeks without seeing an Indian, while in the west, the rivers were like highways. All along the banks of the river were located various Indian tribes, from the Yakimas to the Walla Wallas. The Corps of Discovery stopped to trade food—mostly dogs—from them because Meriwether did not want to lose time sending men out to hunt. Arriving at a village with Chief Twisted Hair, Sacagawea, and Pomp seemed to calm any fears the Indians had about meeting their first white men.

Meriwether and William were single-minded now. They were no longer in the United States but in land whose ownership was disputed among

Britain, Russia, and Spain. Because of this, Meriwether did not have to stop and give his "Welcome
to the United States" speech to the tribes he
encountered. Nor did he have to investigate them
in the same way for Jefferson, though where he
could, he wrote down the vocabulary of the various
tribes in the hope it would aid white traders in the
future.

With the current in their favor, sometimes the
corps covered more than thirty miles a day. On
October 15, the river they had been following
flowed into the Columbia River. The Columbia was
swift and wide, and Meriwether marveled at how
clear the water was. No matter how deep the river
was, he could see clearly to its rocky bottom. As
well, the water teemed with salmon, which were so
abundant that one Indian could easily catch a
hundred a day.

They moved on down the Columbia, sensing
that the Pacific Ocean was not far away now. But
to get to the Pacific they had to pass through some
formidable obstacles in the form of ferocious
rapids. At one point, at a place called The Dalles,
the Columbia River narrowed to only forty-five
yards across. As the full volume of water flowed
through this constriction, it became turbulent and
angry, crashing against the jagged rocks that
restricted its flow. As it boiled and churned, it sent
cascades of frothing spray billowing into the air.

Meriwether and William decided that the rocks
were too jagged to portage their heavy dugout
canoes around this rapid. They would just have to

run it in their canoes and hope they got through. However, essential items like their journals, maps, plant samples, navigation equipment, guns, ammunition, and trade goods were taken out of the canoes and given to the nonswimmers in the group to carry around the rapid.

Seeing what the Corps of Discovery was about to do, the Indians lined up on both sides of the rapid. "Doesn't the white man know that no one has ever taken his canoe through this rapid?" they asked, adding that if they continued, the men would surely all be drowned in the river.

Although Meriwether listened to their concerns, the expedition had no other viable option for getting downriver than to run the rapid. They paddled out into the main channel of the river, and one after another, each canoe headed into the tempest. The canoes pitched and rolled in the thrashing water and thumped over and around jutting rocks and boulders. Spray washed over them, soaking every man to the skin, but they kept paddling.

Much to the Indians' surprise, one by one the canoes emerged triumphant from the spray at the end of the rapid. They had done it. They had made it safely through a rapid that even the Indians refused to negotiate in their canoes.

The corps camped on a rocky outcrop overlooking the river, and the men dried their clothes and luggage before heading downriver again. It was here that Chief Twisted Hair left them. Since the Indians farther downriver no longer spoke the same language, he would be of no use to the corps as interpreter. As well, he feared that the Chinook Indians who lived downriver would kill him if he entered their territory.

Two more ferocious rapids awaited the Corps of Discovery downstream, but the men managed to negotiate them safely. At the bottom of the last rapid, the river once again opened out, and Meriwether thought he began to see signs that the flow of the river was affected by the tide. As well, when he climbed to the top of the cliffs that lined the river, he could see conical mountains rising in the distance on both sides of the river. He immediately recognized these as the mountains Captain Vancouver had marked in the distance on his map of the estuary of the Columbia River. The Corps of Discovery was once again traveling in charted territory. They were back on the map! Everyone in the corps was elated. The men were now very close to their destination.

One thing the men didn't appreciate as they got closer to the coast was the weather. It rained often, and when it didn't rain, they found themselves engulfed in mist. Everything they owned was limp and molding.

As they traveled on, they saw more and more signs of white traders. The Indians were no longer startled by the men's white skin, nor were they dazzled by the corps's trade goods. These Indians wanted to trade for guns and ammunition. As a result, they drove increasingly harder bargains, and Meriwether began to worry they would have little left to live on or trade with by the time they reached the sea.

On the morning of November 7, 1805, the men paddled determinedly onward. Meriwether reasoned they surely didn't have far to go now. The smell of salt was heavy in the air, and the water of the Columbia was so brackish it was undrinkable. Around midday the drizzling rain stopped and the clouds parted. First one man let out a holler of delight, and the others quickly followed. They had done it! There, directly in front of them was the Pacific Ocean.

By dead reckoning along the way, William Clark estimated that the Corps of Discovery had traveled 4,162 miles from the mouth of the Missouri River to become the first Americans to reach the western coast of the North American continent overland. The men puffed out their chests in pride at the achievement. Their excitement, though, was short-lived when the strong tide and high winds forced the canoes ashore at Point Ellice on the north side of the estuary. The men huddled together on a narrow strip of beach, hemmed in from behind by mossy cliffs.

It rained steadily for eleven days, during which time the waters of the Columbia River were too turbulent to canoe across. Meriwether had never seen such rainfall. Storm after storm pounded their soggy, wind-blown outpost, and huge waves dumped enormous uprooted cedar trees dangerously close to camp.

When he first encountered the vibrant coastal forest, Meriwether had marveled at how everything was so lush and green. Now he knew why. It was the result of constant rain. The men watched as their buckskin clothes rotted off their backs, their tents became sodden and useless, and what food they had grew thick with mold in hours. They waited anxiously for the storms to abate so they could round the point and find a sandy beach on the coast. Of course the big question on everyone's mind was, Would there be a ship in the vicinity that could take them back to the East Coast?

Although the foul weather immobilized the Corps of Discovery, the local Clatsop Indians were masters of the waves. They used elaborately decorated, wide, and seaworthy cedar canoes that darted around in and out of the swell. During the time the corps was holed up on the beach, the Indians came to trade fish and roots with them. Meriwether was astonished by their seamanship. There was no way any of his men would venture out in such conditions.

Eventually the storms abated and the swell died down. The Corps of Discovery hurriedly packed their canoes and pushed off from the damp, dreary beach they had been confined to. They followed the north bank of the Columbia River as they paddled toward the open ocean. At Point Chinook they made camp again. From there Meriwether took four men and set out to explore the coast. He was desperate to find a trading ship where he could use the letter of credit that Jefferson had given him and that he had carefully preserved all the way from Washington. With the letter of credit the corps would be able to restock their provision. Meriwether found no ship, however, and after exploring along the beach for several miles and carving his name and the date into a fir tree, he returned to camp disappointed and empty-handed. The Corps of Discovery would have to settle in for a long, wet winter and do the best they could with what they had.

Meriwether later learned from the Indians that no trading ship would arrive at the Columbia River until late spring the following year, when the Indians would have replenished their stockpiles of sea otter pelts to trade for the white man's goods.

The Clatsop Indians also told Meriwether and William that the better supply of wild game was on the south bank of the river. That sounded like a good location to set up camp for the winter, since the hunters could supplement the corps's meager rations with deer and elk meat. However, since the men had endured so much to get to the coast, the co-captains didn't feel they had the right to order a fort be built where they chose. By now the opinion of every member of the corps was valued, so Meriwether and William decided they should vote on where to set up a winter fort. The choices were to remain where they were presently camped, go back upriver to the last set of rapids, and explore the other side of the river before deciding. Everyone except Pomp got to vote, and in the end the majority was in favor of exploring the south bank of the river.

Once they crossed the river, it took about a week to find a suitable location for their winter camp. The site was about three miles up a tributary river—which they named the Lewis and Clark River—on a small bluff that rose about thirty feet above the high-tide mark. A spring was nearby, as were plenty of tall fir trees to build a log fort with and to provide firewood. The site was only a few miles from the ocean, where Meriwether hoped to extract salt from seawater. Everyone on the expedition, except William Clark, liked his food well salted, and the men had run out of salt some time ago. Most promising of all, George Drouillard killed six elk and five deer near the site.

On December 7, 1805, the men began building Fort Clatsop. The fort was a sturdy affair, much like Fort Mandan, which they had built the winter before. Rain, punctuated by sleet and lightning, fell constantly throughout the building process. With very little clothing to protect them and dripping wet bedding, everyone was anxious to be inside as soon as possible. As a result the building of the fort progressed rapidly.

The Christmas of 1805 was not nearly as comfortable as the one the Corps of Discovery had spent the year before among the Mandan Indians. Although the group was now finally housed inside the fort out of the rain, it was nearly impossible to keep a fire lit, and everything continued to be damp. The meat tainted overnight, and the roots Sacagawea gathered began to rot as soon as they were dug up. The local Indians came to barter, but they had inflated ideas about how much their wares were worth. Soon the corps had all but run out of items to trade.

Small groups of men regularly made the trek to the ocean to make salt. They accomplished this by boiling large pots of salt water until the water evaporated, leaving the salt caked to the sides of the pot. The salt-making teams came back to the fort with wonderful tales of seeing dolphins and whales swimming just offshore. Sacagawea had never seen the ocean before, and she marveled at its vast expanse.

Meriwether and William spent a lot of their time at the desks Joseph Field had fashioned for them. William devoted his energy to drawing maps of where they had been, and Meriwether sketched and wrote long descriptions of the plants and animals he had encountered along the way.

The co-captains weren't the only ones writing during this time. Five other members of the corps, the three sergeants and two privates, kept personal journals of the expedition and used the time to bring them up to date and add further description of all they had seen and experienced so far.

The elk and deer, which had been plentiful at first, were soon all hunted and killed. Once again obtaining an adequate supply of food became a problem. By early March 1806 the corps were hungry, and they had nothing left to trade for food. Thoughts began to turn eastward. Meriwether and William agreed it was time to go home.

No ships had been spotted over the winter, and it was too risky to wait until late spring when the Indians said they would return, in case they didn't arrive or they didn't have room to transport the Corps of Discovery back to the East Coast of the United States. Meriwether decided they would have to return the way they had come, up over the Rocky Mountains and across the Great Plains.

For this undertaking the men needed two new canoes to replace some that had been damaged on the way down the Columbia River. However, they had little to barter for the canoes. Since they needed to leave a few items in store for the return trip, Meriwether traded whatever goods he could for one canoe but was unable to pay the high price the Indians demanded for the other.

Frustrated and desperate, Meriwether did something he had never done before and hoped he would never have to do again. He ordered several of the men to steal a canoe from the Indians.

On March 23, 1806, Meriwether Lewis closed the gate to Fort Clatsop for the last time, and the members of the Corps of Discovery climbed into their canoes. For the first time in over two years, they were headed east into the rising sun.

Chapter 16

Homeward Bound

The salmon were due to run upriver at any time, and thousands of Indians were camped along the banks of the Columbia, waiting for their share of the fish. While they waited they had little to do, and the arrival of white men in canoes promised them some harmless fun.

From the time the Corps of Discovery departed Fort Clatsop until they left the river at The Dalles and set out overland twenty-nine days later, the Indians constantly harassed them. Anything that wasn't nailed or tied down was stolen, including Meriwether's dog Scannon. Three of the men went in search of the dog. They retrieved him from the robbers and returned him to camp. By then axes and tomahawks had been stolen. All of them, the Indians and the members of the corps, were cold, wet, and hungry. And with so much frustration over the constant thievery, the atmosphere was ripe for disaster. Somehow Meriwether and William managed to keep the men's resentment at bay, and the situation did not explode into violence.

It was tough going upriver against the current. Sometimes they had to push the canoes; at other times they towed them through the lesser rapids with elk-skin rope. At the major rapids they had no option but to portage their luggage and canoes around them. When they reached The Dalles, rather than portage around this set of rapids, they decided to abandon their canoes. They traded for some horses from a local band of Indians and set out overland for the Nez Perce Indians. The horses did not come cheap, though. The men had to part with their large cooking pot, leaving themselves with only four small pots for the rest of the journey back.

Meriwether was relieved to leave the Indian tribes of the Columbia River behind and was delighted when on April 24 they arrived at a Walla Walla village. Yellept, the village chief, enthusiastically greeted the Corps of Discovery. He had met them on their journey west and was eager to host them on their way back.

Thankfully, the Walla Walla were entirely different from the Indian tribes farther downriver. They respected the corps's property and willingly supplied the men with fish and wood for fuel. Chief Yellept had a Shoshone slave, and using her to interpret from Walla Walla into Shoshone so that Sacagawea could translate, Meriwether was able to obtain a great deal of useful information, including the fact that there was a shortcut to the western end of the Lolo Trail.

That night the Walla Wallas threw a huge party for everyone. Over 550 men, women, and children danced first to their own drums and then to the unfamiliar sound of Pierre Cruzatte's fiddle. The mood was lighthearted. The members of the corps felt they were back among people they trusted.

When the expedition set out from the village two days later, they followed a shortcut that cut eighty miles from the route they had taken downriver on the way west. This was a good thing because the weather was horrendous. Sometimes it rained, other times it hailed or snowed, but always something wet was falling from the sky. They were all eager to get back to the plains, where they could finally dry out.

On May 5 the Corps of Discovery arrived at Chief Twisted Hair's village. The chief was out with a hunting party, but the Nez Perce made the corps welcome. The Nez Perce were particularly pleased to see William Clark. Although Meriwether acted as the corps's doctor, it was William who had made the medical impression when he passed through the village on the way west. At that time he had rubbed linament on an old Indian man's sore knee, which began to feel much better. The story of this powerful medicine had been told repeatedly over the winter, and as soon as William appeared, many of the Nez Perce began begging him to take a look at their ailments.

William set about treating the Indians' ailments as best he could while Meriwether talked with the lesser chiefs through a convoluted chain of interpreters. The chiefs gave Meriwether some bad news. The snow had been unusually deep during the past winter, and the Indians predicted that the mountains would not be ready to cross until the Corps of Discovery had slept one and one-half moons among the Nez Perce. Meriwether added it up. One and one-half moons was forty-five days! There was no way he was willing to wait that long. However, he did concede that it was not practical to begin passage over the mountains just yet. One look up at the snow-covered peaks was enough to confirm that.

Meriwether took readings from the river every morning, waiting for it to swell with melting snow from the highlands. On May 17 he wrote in his journal, "I am pleased at finding the river rise so rapidly, it no doubt is attributable to the melting snows of the mountains; that icy barier which seperates me from my friends and Country, from all which makes life esteemable. Patience, patience."

Patience was surely what the Corps of Discovery needed. To keep the men's minds occupied, Meriwether organized competitions between the men and the Indians. The men ran horse races and foot races, held archery and shooting tournaments, and played endless games of quoits. These activities, along with hunting for food, filled up the men's time. But still their thoughts would wander to the journey ahead.

On June 3 Meriwether heard that a young Indian boy had been dispatched over the pass to gather information about how the tribes on the other side of the mountains had fared through the winter. When Meriwether asked the chiefs whether they thought it was time for the corps to be on its way, the chiefs said it should wait another half a moon before setting out. Half a month was too long for Meriwether. In the valley where they were camped, spring was bursting out all around them. If a lone young Indian could make it over the mountains, so could his men. Meriwether and William announced to the men that a month was long enough to wait and it was time to be on their way.

By now the Corps of Discovery had sixty horses. This included the horses they had left with the Nez Perce the previous fall and some that William had received for his medical services. This meant that each member of the corps had a horse to ride and almost all of them a packhorse to trail behind. It was with an air of optimism that the expedition set out on the morning of June 10. Even the freezing, driving rain did not dampen the men's spirits. Nothing was better than being on the way again, and Meriwether was determined to be back in the United States as soon as possible.

The first leg of the journey was relatively easy. The men rode their horses across the Weippe Prairie and on June 15 started to climb the looming mountains. By now Meriwether was scanning the trail for the two Indian guides who had promised to catch up with the corps and lead them over Lolo Pass. It was raining hard, and the men and horses slipped and fell over the fallen trees that lay across the trail. All around them were signs of spring: the unfolding leaves of honeysuckle, huckle-berries, and other plants, all of which Meriwether wrote about in his journal.

The following day, as they climbed higher, the wet spring weather gave way to brutal winter. Eleven feet of snow covered the trail. The men became numb with cold, and the horses did not have any grass to eat. And worst of all, they still had six days of travel ahead of them to cross the mountains.

For the first time since setting out on the expe-dition, Meriwether and William began talking about turning back. The more they talked about it, the more they knew it was the right choice to make. With no guide, little food, and no grass for the horses to graze, it was madness to go on. They turned around. Discouraged and disappointed they made their way back to the Nez Perce.

Nine days later, they set out again. This time five teenage Indian boys accompanied them as guides. The snow was melting fast and was down from eleven feet thick to only seven. Despite this, the Indian boys were able to guide the corps to grassy meadows where the horses could graze. Meriwether was impressed with the boys' knowl-edge of the mountains. It made all the difference, and they made it to the other side in only six days, five days shorter than the route Old Toby had taken them on.

The men were almost euphoric as they made their way down the final slope of the mountains. The worst of the journey home was behind them, or so they thought.

Once they were across the mountains, Meriwether ordered three days' rest for everyone, though he and William busied themselves planning the next leg of the journey. Rather than return exactly the way they had come, the co-captains decided to make maximum use of their time to explore and map more land. To accomplish this, the Corps of Discovery would split up.

William agreed to take twenty-one men and Sacagawea and head for Camp Fortunate, where they had left their canoes and a cache of supplies. Once they had the canoes and supplies, they would make their way down the Jefferson River to Three Forks. There William's group would split into three. Sergeant Nathaniel Pryor would lead two men overland to the Mandan Indians in the hope they could find a trader there who could convince the Sioux chiefs to return to Washington with the Corps of Discovery. Eight men and Sacagawea would set out to follow the course of the Yellowstone River on horseback until it was possible to build boats and float downstream to join the Missouri River. Meanwhile the remainder of the men would take the canoes and follow the Missouri River to the Great Falls and portage around them.

While they were doing this, the five Nez Perce teenagers would lead Meriwether and nine men along their buffalo-hunting route to the Great

Falls. From there they would head north and try to find the headwaters of the Marias River. Meriwether had fond hopes that this would take him all the way into Canada, in which case he could report to Jefferson that the Louisiana Purchase encompassed some British land. When he had finished exploring, Meriwether would meet the group with the canoes at the Great Falls and help in portaging them. They would then float on down the Missouri River to join up with William and the rest of the Corps of Discovery.

On the map it was five hundred miles in a straight line from where they were camped to the confluence of the Missouri and Yellowstone Rivers, where they were to meet up again. Of course, Meriwether and William anticipated traveling twice that far as they followed the twists and turns of trails and rivers. They estimated it would take about six weeks for them to cover their various routes and rendezvous at the spot they had chosen

Meriwether Lewis and William Clark separated on July 3, 1806. The following morning the five Nez Perce boys who had been such able guides refused to go on any farther. According to them the trail was well beaten and easy to follow, and they were petrified of venturing into Blackfoot Indian territory.

Meriwether was aware of the Nez Perce's great fear and distrust of Blackfoot Indians, and so he did not force the issue. He gave the boys all the meat they had and reluctantly said good-bye. It was a sad parting. The Nez Perce had helped feed, guide, and supply horses to the Corps of Discovery. Everyone on the expedition was in their debt. As the boys left, they warned the men to be wary of the Blackfeet and not to trust them. Meriwether assured the boys all would be well. After all, the men had strong horses and plenty of guns.

It was July 4 when the Nez Perce guides left, but Meriwether did not order any patriotic celebration that day as he had in previous years.

Five days later Meriwether and his men were feasting on roast buffalo, which tasted even better than they had remembered. It was good to once again have an abundant supply of meat.

As they made their way along the trail toward the Great Falls, the men were on the lookout for Indians. With each passing day Meriwether became a little less confident about his plan to meet with the Blackfeet. What if they were as vicious and unpredictable as the Nez Perce said they were? It would be dangerous for the men if they were. He remembered their narrow escape from the Sioux the year before. He began to wonder whether it might be better not to meet with the Blackfoot Indians to give them his "Welcome to the United States" speech.

As it happened, their first experience with the Blackfeet did not involve a meeting at all. In fact, the men did not even see the Indians as they circled their camp late on the night of July 10 and made off with seven of their seventeen horses. It was a bitter blow to Meriwether the next morning, since it meant he would have to change his plans. They needed more than one horse apiece to travel up the Marias River. Later that day, as they reached the head of the Great Falls, Meriwether was still pondering what to do. Like a fork in a river, he had two directions he could follow. He could keep all the men together and head for the rendezvous with William. Or he could take fewer men than planned and head up the Marias to explore, leaving the rest of the men to help portage the canoes when they arrived, and then meet William at the mouth of the Marias River.

Which course should he take? He wasn't sure, and he did not have William Clark to discuss the options with. Finally he decided on the second option and chose Joseph Field and his brother Reuben and George Drouillard to go with him. That night around the campfire, Meriwether told the men of the change in plan.

On July 16, Meriwether, the Field brothers, and George Drouillard, along with six horses and Scannon trotting behind, headed northward into Blackfoot country to explore the upper reaches of the Marias River. Meriwether had warned the men to be on constant alert, never more than an arm's length away from their rifles.

A week later, on July 23, as the four men made camp, Meriwether dubbed it Camp Disappointment, since that was exactly what he felt. The Marias River was just a trickle now, and he felt sure they were miles from the 49th parallel that marked the Canadian border. Still, having come this far, he decided to take some celestial readings and accurately fix their location. The weather did not cooperate, however. It was drizzly and overcast for one day, and then for another and another. As Meriwether waited for the sky to clear, he tried to keep his nervousness in check. He knew that at any moment Blackfoot warriors could gallop up, and by now he had dismissed the idea of a friendly meeting with them. After three days of waiting for the weather to improve, Meriwether gave up, and on July 26 he and the three men headed back crosscountry to meet up with the canoes.

The men stopped to eat around midday at the river's edge. Two hours later, when they had eaten and rested, it was decided that Drouillard would ride down the edge of the river while the other three men rode up on top of the bluff that ran along the river. They had just reached the top of the bluff when Meriwether stopped short and gestured for Reuben and Joseph to get back.

There were Indians ahead who had about thirty horses with them. Meriwether focused his telescope on the Indians and counted. Five, six, seven, eight warriors, all staring intently down at the river below. They had spotted Drouillard.

For a brief moment the possibility of abandoning Drouillard and skirting around the band of Indians flitted through Meriwether's mind, but he could never do that. Somehow he would have to figure out a way to rescue his best tracker and get the men safely to the rendezvous point.

The Last Leg of the Journey

"We'll have to make the best of it, men," Meriwether said. "Let's advance slowly."

Scannon gave a low growl as the men rode out from the cover of the bushes they had been hiding among. Within seconds one of the Blackfoot warriors yelled, and the eyes of all the Indians were soon fixed on the three men.

"Steady. Let's not make any sudden moves," Meriwether instructed.

A war cry pierced the air, and one of the warriors galloped at full speed toward the white men. Instinctively Meriwether swung his leg over and slipped off his horse. He stood and waited, holding his open palms in front of him. The young warrior came within yards of Meriwether and then whipped his horse's head around and galloped back to the other warriors.

Meriwether got back on his horse and slowly advanced toward the Indians. Grave thoughts ran through his head. There were eight warriors on horses, but a number of the other horses they had with them were bridled. Were there other warriors? And if so, where? Behind them, perhaps? Meriwether felt the hairs on the back of his neck rise, but he did not turn around. The worst thing he could do was show fear.

The Indians' and the white men's eyes locked as the distance between them narrowed. Two of the warriors were armed with guns, and the rest had bows and arrows and tomahawks. Eventually Meriwether motioned the Field brothers to stop, and once again he dismounted. Slowly and cautiously he walked toward the Indians. To his surprise, they too dismounted and greeted him using sign language. By now Meriwether had picked up a few simple words of sign language from Drouillard, and he signed back. Soon he understood that the Indians were asking for tobacco to smoke.

Meriwether thought of Drouillard below at the river's edge hunting for food, totally oblivious to what was happening above him. Somehow he had to find a way to get Drouillard back with them. A plan rushed into his mind, and using the best signing he could, Meriwether explained that their hunter had the tobacco and pipe with him.

The Blackfeet seemed to understand, so Meriwether kept going. He suggested that Reuben and one of the warriors go down to the river and bring Drouillard back. They could then all smoke together.

The Indians took the bait, and Reuben and a warrior were quickly dispatched.

By now it was late afternoon, and Meriwether feared the Blackfeet had no intention of letting them leave. He decided it was better for them to all stay together for the night. At least that way he would know where the Indians were. So he asked the Blackfeet if they would like to camp together for the night. The Indians nodded, and so began one of the longest nights of Meriwether Lewis's life.

Drouillard and Reuben rejoined the group, and they built a fire together. Both sides watched every move the other made. The Indians gathered sticks and shaped them into a dome and then threw a large buffalo hide over it to make a crude tent. They invited the men to sleep in it with them. Meriwether and Drouillard agreed, although the Field brothers preferred to stay by the fire. The Indians smoked until about eight that night and then climbed into their tent to sleep. Everyone, both Indian and white man, slept with his weapon held tightly in his hand.

Meriwether stood guard for the first watch, keeping his eyes peeled lest the Blackfeet try to harm them or rob them during the night. At 11 P.M. he woke Joseph to take the next watch. Meriwether then crept into the buffalo skin tent and lay down. He gripped his rifle and fought to keep his eyes open, listening for any strange noises. As hard as he tried to stay awake, his weary body soon descended into sleep.

"Let go of my gun!" Meriwether awoke with a start and looked around in the dawn light. To his left Drouillard was wrenching his gun back from one of the Indians. Meriwether reached for his rifle, but it was gone. Instinctively he reached for his pistol and leapt out from under the buffalo skin tent.

Outside a Blackfoot warrior was running away carrying Meriwether's rifle. Urgently Meriwether signaled for him to lay down the rifle or he would shoot. The Indian understood. He bent down and placed the rifle on the ground as Reuben and Joseph raced up.

"We've got him!" Joseph yelled as he and his brother raised their rifles and aimed at the Indian.

"Don't shoot," Meriwether ordered. "He's doing what I asked."

After a moment of calm, mayhem broke out. "They're after the horses!" Drouillard yelled.

Meriwether's heart froze. Without horses they would never make it back to the river in time, if they made it at all. "Get them! Shoot if you have to!" he ordered as he ran toward two Blackfoot warriors. Drouillard and the Field brothers sprinted in the opposite direction after the main party of Indians.

Soon Meriwether was on his own, racing after two Indians and three horses. They all came to a place where the bluff was too steep for the horses to descend.

"Give me back the horses or I'll shoot," Meriwether ordered. The warriors, who crouched behind a rock for cover, might not have understood his words, but with his rifle cocked and aimed, Meriwether was sure they understood his intentions.

Suddenly one of the warriors jumped out from behind a rock and aimed his musket at Meriwether. Meriwether steadied his rifle as his finger closed on the trigger. *Bang!* The warrior fell to his knees just as his musket discharged. Meriwether felt the bullet whisk past his head. Since Meriwether didn't have his powder pouch with him, he could not reload his rifle. He darted behind a tree and then ran back to camp, arriving just ahead of Drouillard.

"Where are the other two?" Meriwether asked between pants.

"Down in the valley. I lost sight of them," Drouillard replied.

"Let's get some of these horses bridled and go find them," Meriwether said. He was referring to the Blackfeet's own horses, which they had left unattended while they ran off on foot with the white men's horses.

Within minutes the men had four horses bridled and were about to ride off when Joseph and Reuben Field rode up on their own horses and towed two more behind them.

"Let's get out of here. I stabbed a warrior in the heart!" Reuben yelled.

"First you men load up the horses, and I'll throw everything of theirs on the fire," Meriwether said. He began heaving the Indians' shields and bows and arrows into the dying embers of the fire.

Orange flames flared. By the time Meriwether was done, the other men had loaded three packhorses. The four men quickly mounted their horses and, with the three packhorses in tow, galloped off. Heads down, they raced for their lives. They had to get to the Missouri River and the canoes before a band of irate Blackfoot Indians hunted them down.

Finally, as the sun climbed higher in the sky, Meriwether signaled for the men to slow their horses to a gentle canter. Neither the horses nor the men could keep up such a breakneck pace indefinitely.

By nightfall they had covered eighty miles, but they pressed on through the night, too fearful to camp, alert to every sound. At 2 A.M. men and horses could go no farther, and Meriwether ordered a halt. The men tethered their horses and lay down on the grass to sleep.

At first light Meriwether staggered to his feet. His body was so sore he could barely scramble onto his horse. The other three men were suffering from the same complaint, but they all needed to keep riding—their lives depended on it.

Off they galloped again. Two hours later they heard a gunshot, and then another. Meriwether motioned for the men to stop. They listened. Was it Indians? Finally, on full alert, they urged their horses forward on over a hill. A wonderful sight greeted them on the other side. It was the Missouri River, and floating down it were the canoes Sergeant Ordway and his men had portaged around the Great Falls. It was they who had fired the shots.

The timing was perfect. Meriwether fired a shot back, and within minutes the two groups were reunited. The men deposited their luggage and supplies into the canoe and climbed in, leaving the horses on the riverbank. Now that they were safe, Meriwether felt the energy drain from his body. He had ridden 120 miles in the past twenty-four hours, all on raw nervous energy.

A short distance downriver they stopped and recovered the cache of supplies they had buried on the island in the mouth of the Marias River on the way west. With the supplies aboard, they set off again. The current whisked them along, and some times they covered seventy miles a day. Fourteen days later, on August 12, the entire Corps of Discovery was reunited downstream from the mouth of the Yellowstone River.

That night everyone swapped adventure stories around the campfire. Nathaniel Pryor and the two men who were supposed to head overland to the Mandan Indians explained how their horses had been stolen on the second day of their trek. They had no choice but to abandon their mission, make bull boats, and head downriver after William Clark. William told of coming across a herd of buffalo so large that they had to beach their canoes and wait more than half an hour while the beasts swam across the river ahead. William also praised Sacagawea. A long time ago she had become a valued member of the corps, and she proved her worth again as she guided the men over terrain that was familiar to her.

As he listened to the stories, Meriwether lay facedown on a buffalo skin. He had one more tale to tell. It was the story of how a week before he and Pierre Cruzatte had gone out hunting. Along the way the near-sighted Cruzatte had mistaken Meriwether for an elk and shot him in the buttocks. As a result, Meriwether unceremoniously became the only member of the Corps of Discovery to reenter civilization with a gunshot wound.

The wound was actually very painful, and it kept Meriwether lying facedown in the bottom of the canoe as they sped downriver towards the Mandan.

It was a scorching afternoon on August 14 when the Corps of Discovery arrived back at Fort Mandan, or more precisely the site where it had stood. The fort had burned down in an accidental fire. Meriwether felt immense satisfaction as he steadied himself and hobbled out of the canoe to greet Chief Big White. It had been four and a half months since the corps had left Fort Clatsop on the Pacific Coast, and in that time they had journeyed 1,950 miles over every imaginable terrain. Despite the dangers they had faced, not a single man had been lost.

There was singing and dancing at the Mandan village that night. The next morning Private John Colter asked Meriwether and William if he could be discharged from the Corps of Discovery so that he could head west again to trap fur. The co-captains agreed, and along with a gun and ammunition, they gave him all the food they could spare. The expedition that had forged a diverse group of rugged individuals into a tight-knit team was now all but over. Getting the rest of the men to St. Louis and the priceless maps, journals, and specimens they had collected to Washington was all that remained for Meriwether Lewis and William Clark to do.

At the Mandan village the Corps of Discovery also bid farewell to Toussaint Charbonneau, Sacagawea, and Pomp. It was a sad parting. The men owed so much to Sacagawea and her skills as a food gatherer, guide, and interpreter. Little Pomp, who was now eighteen months old, stood beside his mother and waved good-bye to the men.

Not everything about departing the Mandan village was sad. Meriwether had convinced Chief Big White to come with them to Washington to meet the Great Chief of the Seventeen Great Nations of America. Accompanying Chief Big White on the trip were his wife and son and a French interpreter and his wife and two children. So although the corps left four people behind, it picked up seven more for the last leg of the journey.

The Corps of Discovery's next stop was the Arikara village, where the Indians were anxiously awaiting news of their leader, Chief Ankedoucharo. Following Meriwether's advice, the chief had gone to Washington to visit, and he had not yet returned. Meriwether assured the Arikara that he would find the chief and make sure he was returned safely to them.

After smoking a peace pipe with the Arikara, the corps moved on again. Not far downriver they met up with Joseph Gravelines and Pierre Dorian, who were on a grim mission. They had been sent to tell the Arikara Indians that Chief Ankedoucharo was not coming back. He was dead. This news sent a shudder down Meriwether's spine. Even though Joseph Gravelines assured Meriwether that the chief had died of natural causes, Meriwether wondered whether the Arikara would believe that.

There was more news too, most of it political. Thomas Jefferson had been reelected in a landslide victory that had shattered the Federalists. And there was the shocking tale of the Burr-Hamilton duel. Aaron Burr, the vice president and a man Meriwether knew well, had been deeply insulted by fellow politician Alexander Hamilton. In a fit of southern pride, Burr challenged Hamilton to a duel to defend his honor. The duel took place in July 1804, and Burr had shot Hamilton to death. Now, two years later, George Clinton was vice president, and Aaron Burr, along with sixty supporters, was holed up on an island in the upper Ohio River. To Meriwether it sounded like the plot to a novel, and he was anxious to hear all the details from the president himself.

The closer the Corps of Discovery got to civilization, the more anxious the men became to get home. The men suggested the co-captains stop sending out hunters, which slowed down progress. Instead they offered to eat the wild fruits and berries that grew along the riverbank. Although they had no more meat to eat, they covered an extra ten or twenty miles a day.

As the men made their way down the Missouri River, they paddled through Sioux territory. They expected trouble but found none. Perhaps the Teton Sioux were off hunting buffalo, but not a single Indian came to the water's edge to watch them pass, let alone ambush them. Meriwether hoped the keelboat had fared as well on its way downriver the year before.

They passed the bluffs where two years before they had met with the Yankton Sioux, and then farther downstream they stopped at Floyd's Bluff, where Meriwether paid his respects at Sergeant Charles Floyd's gravesite. Floyd was the only man they had lost on the expedition.

Downstream from the bluffs they encountered more and more fur trappers and traders headed upriver. And each group they encountered celebrated the corps's return with whiskey and their best food. The men, who had not had any alcohol or fresh rations in fifteen months, were happy to be showered with food and drink. They savored the taste of chocolate and sugar and biscuits dripping with blackberry jelly.

Farther downriver they passed a herd of cattle and began to notice outlying cabins along the riverbank that had not been there when they left. The men's excitement grew. They would soon be back in St. Louis.

On September 23, 1806, the Corps of Discovery pulled their canoes ashore one last time. They had made it back to St. Louis after a two-and-a-half-year absence. The people of St. Louis rushed to meet them and carried the men to the city square. A widespread rumor that everyone on the expedition had been killed fueled the enthusiastic welcome.

Chapter 18

Pomp, Ceremony, and Frustration

Meriwether Lewis had one goal when he reached St. Louis, and that was to alert the president of his return. Much to his delight the keelboat had made it safely downriver to St. Louis the previous summer, and its cargo had been shipped to Washington. As a result, the letter he had sent back on the boat had already been published and was available as far away as Germany. Meriwether dipped his quill and wrote, "It is with pleasure that I announce to you the safe arrival of myself and my party at 12 o'clock today at this place with our papers and baggage."

From there the letter went on for page after page outlining the route the expedition had taken to the Pacific Ocean and back, the Indian tribes they had encountered along the way, and some of the strange and wonderful animals and plants Meriwether had cataloged. Meriwether also told the president as diplomatically as he could that there was no all-water route that joined the Missouri River to the Columbia. Wishful thinking would have to give way to reality. It was 340 miles from the headwaters of the Missouri River to the head-waters of the Columbia River—and not just any 340 miles! Meriwether reported that 200 miles of it was along a "good road" but the other 140 miles was "the most formidable part of the track...[over] tremendious mountains which for 60 miles are covered with eternal snows."

Meriwether then went on to tell Jefferson that he was heading straight for Albemarle County in the hope that his mother was still alive. After sign-ing his name, he added one more sentence to the letter. "The whole of the party who accompanied me from the Mandans have returned in good health, which is not, I assure you, to me one of the least pleasant considerations of this voyage."

Meriwether would have liked to send William Clark's maps to the president as well, since he knew how anxious Jefferson would be to receive them, but he decided against it. The maps were too precious to consign to the mail.

Once the letter to the president was dispatched, it was time to celebrate. On the afternoon and evening of September 25, St. Louis threw a huge ball in honor of the Corps of Discovery. The tables at the event burgeoned with delicious food, and pretty women vied for dances with the suntanned explorers. Seventeen toasts were proposed, and everyone in attendance drank heartily.

Meriwether had more parties to attend, newspaper articles to write, and new clothes to purchase before he set off for home on November 4. He did not travel alone. Along with Chief Big White and his entourage, William Clark, York, Sergeants Gass and Ordway, and Privates Labiche and Frazier traveled with him.

Their arrival in Louisville, Kentucky, was met with great fanfare. Bonfires blazed through the night, and music reverberated in the streets. It was the same in every town they passed through. They were met with seeming endless rounds of questions, toasts, and banquets. When they reached Frankfort, Kentucky, the group split up. Meriwether and Chief Big White and his entourage headed for Charlottesville, Virginia; the others went their own ways. William confided that he was headed to Fincastle, Virginia, to visit a young woman named Julia Hancock, after whom he had named the Judith River. He wanted to tell her of the river's name himself and perhaps do some courting.

December 13 was a cold Monday, but Meriwether could not have cared less. He was home at Locust Hill, sitting in front of the fire talking with his mother and brother. His family was very proud of his exploits.

Meriwether and Chief Big White and his group stayed at Locust Hill for Christmas 1806. As much as he enjoyed regaling family and friends with stories of the journey, Meriwether was anxious to see

President Jefferson in Washington. Three days after Christmas, he and Chief Big White set out again over frozen roads. It was three and a half years since Meriwether had last seen the capital city.

New Year's Day 1807 was all Meriwether had hoped it would be. President Jefferson received Meriwether and the others with enough pomp and ceremony to awe the Mandan chief. As Jefferson gave a welcome speech, Meriwether thought back to the previous New Year's Day, when the men were damp and hungry at Fort Clatsop. Now, looking at the smile on the president's face, Meriwether knew it had all been worth it.

Over the next several days President Jefferson cancelled his appointments so that he could pump all the information he could from Meriwether. Meriwether produced William Clark's map, and the two men got down on their hands and knees to examine it. Jefferson wanted to know everything about the plants, animals, rivers, Indians, and weather they had encountered along the way. His curiosity was endless.

The group stayed at the president's house through the winter. While in Washington, Meriwether needed to make sure the government properly rewarded the men on the expedition. On February 28, 1807, the Senate passed a bill giving Meriwether Lewis and William Clark each 1,600 acres of land in Louisiana, while the other men received 320 acres each plus double the pay they were due. There was also something else for Meriwether: The president nominated him to be governor of the Territory of Louisiana.

Meriwether was very pleased with the appointment, and even more so when Jefferson informed him that William was to have the new position of Superintendent of Indian Affairs for Louisiana Territory. Both men would be situated in St. Louis, and they would be a team once again.

William arrived in Washington to accept the position. However, he stayed only a few days. He was eager to get on with his first task, that of getting Chief Big White and his party back to the Mandans. Meriwether promised to travel to St. Louis as soon as he had finished putting his journals in order. This proved to be a huge task, one that Meriwether eventually found overwhelming. Far from just handing his journals over to a publisher, Meriwether had to edit them, prepare plates of the maps, and supervise the drawing of pictures of hundreds of plants and animals from his sketches. Not only did he have to do all of this work, he also had to raise $4,500 to get the journals, which he planned to release in three volumes, printed. Meriwether also spoke at several gatherings of the American Philosophical Society, which had made him a member while he was away.

All this took time—time that Meriwether should have spent in St. Louis in his new role as governor. In fact, it was thirteen months from the time he was given the appointment to the time Meriwether actually arrived in St. Louis. Even then, his journals were not ready for publication.

The St. Louis that Meriwether returned to was very different from the one he had passed through on his way to Washington. The West was rapidly opening up, whether the president wanted it to or not. Groups of people vied for land and influence. Indians were coming to town in increasing numbers looking for work or justice or to cause mayhem. John Jacob Astor and his newly formed American Fur Company sent trappers and traders upriver into the heart of Louisiana Territory, only to end up in conflict with the Indians and British fur traders.

The only bright spot in the situation was that William was at Meriwether's side again. By now he had married Julia Hancock, and they soon had a baby boy, whom they named Meriwether Lewis Clark.

Meriwether did the best he could under the circumstances, but it was impossible to keep the Indian tribes from fighting one another, the British out of Louisiana, and pioneers from squatting on Indian land. By July 1809, the situation was reaching a crisis point. Late in 1807 Nathaniel Pryor had led an expedition up the Missouri River to return Chief Big White and his entourage to Mandan territory. Along the way, Arikara Indians had attacked the convoy, killing three soldiers and wounding eight others, including George Shannon, who had to have his leg amputated. The group fled back downriver to St. Louis, where Chief Big White still waited to be returned to his people.

Also, the Great Osage Indians were at war with the Little Osage Indians, which made passage up the Osage River impossible. And of course, thanks to the increased presence of traders, the Indians now had more guns than ever before.

After carefully thinking over Chief Big White's plight, Meriwether signed a contract with the St. Louis Missouri River Fur Company to escort the chief and his group home at last. The deal cost the government seven thousand dollars, in part because the contract called for the fur company to provide 125 militiamen deemed necessary to guarantee safe passage home for Chief Big White. Once they had delivered the chief to his village, Meriwether gave the traders permission to hunt and trade all the way up the Yellowstone River. He also promised not to issue licenses to anyone else, so that the St. Louis Missouri River Fur Company would have the trading rights to itself. He sent a request to Washington to cover the costs of the mission, along with a bill for five hundred dollars, money Meriwether had used to buy gifts for the Indians the group met along the way.

Meriwether's timing could not have been worse. Although it was normal for the federal government to reimburse him for costs, this time it balked. A war between the United States and the British was brewing, and all the military resources of the country were focused on the Atlantic Ocean. The United States also had a new president, James Madison, who did not appreciate the importance of getting the Mandan chief home at any cost.

In August Meriwether received devastating news. It came in the form of a letter from the new secretary of war, and it coldly informed him that the government would not be reimbursing him the five hundred dollars for Indian gifts and that it was looking into whether it should pay the seven thousand dollars as well. Since this money had already been spent, this left Meriwether to pay the huge bill himself.

Meriwether knew there was only one thing to do. He had to go to Washington and explain the situation to the new administration. On September 3, 1809, Meriwether set out for Washington, accompanied by his servant John Pernier, a freed black slave. Along the way Major James Neelly and his servant joined him on the journey. They rode horses eastward along the Natchez Trace. On Monday, October 9, they crossed the Tennessee River and set up camp. During the night two of the horses strayed, and James Neelly went in search of them. Meanwhile, Meriwether, Pernier, and Neelly's servant rode on, trusting that the major would catch up to them, with or without the two missing horses.

That night Meriwether did not have to camp because they came across a log cabin inn owned by the Grinder family. Located seventy-two miles southwest of Nashville, the inn was a simple affair: The two servants slept in the barn, while Meriwether was given an outside room. Major Neelly did not show up, and Meriwether went to bed around eleven o'clock.

Three hours later, two shots rang out, and Meriwether lay dying. He called out for help, but no one came to his aid as his life drained from him. Meriwether was thirty-five years old when he died.

At noon the following day, the body of Meriwether Lewis was hastily laid to rest in a shallow grave a few yards from Grinder's Inn. No government official visited the scene, and no investigation into his death was ordered. Mrs. Grinder convinced anyone who asked that Meriwether had committed suicide. But had he? The answer to the question remains uncertain to this day. At first everyone believed that Meriwether had killed himself, but as time went on, some people began to have doubts. Mrs. Grinder kept changing her story of what happened, and some of the items Meriwether had with him at the time he died were never found. Ironically, the man who had sought to solve one of the United States' great mysteries—what lay in the unknown land beyond the young nation's western boundary—himself left us a great mystery in his death.

Postscript

Meriwether never finished preparing his journals for publication, and it was left to William Clark to see them through to publication five years later. (The project was delayed because of the War of 1812.)

In 1813 William Clark was appointed governor of the newly established Missouri Territory. He remained Superintendent of Indian Affairs at St. Louis until his death in 1838.

Ambrose, Stephen E. *Undaunted Courage: Meriwether Lewis, Thomas Jefferson, and the Opening of the American West.* Touchstone Books, 1996.

Dillon, Richard. *Meriwether Lewis: A Biography.* Coward-McCann, 1965.

Lewis, Meriwether, and Clark, William, ed. by Elliott Coues. *The History of the Lewis and Clark Expedition* (in three volumes). Dover Publications.

Schmidt, Timothy, and Schmidt, Jeremy. *The Saga of Lewis and Clark: Into the Uncharted West.* DK Publishing, 1999.

About the Authors

Janet and Geoff Benge are a husband and wife writing team with over sixteen years of writing experience. Janet is a former elementary school teacher. Geoff holds a degree in history. Together they have a passion to make history come alive for a new generation of readers.

Originally from New Zealand, the Benges make their home in the Orlando, Florida, area.